Grace Upon Grace
Savouring the Spiritual Exercises through the Arts

MARLENE MARBURG

MORNING STAR PUBLISHING

Published by Morning Star Publishing
P. O. Box 462
Reservoir Vic. 3073
Australia

ISBN 9780648453864

Copyright © Marlene Marburg, 2019.

All rights reserved. Other than for the purposes and subject to the conditions prescribed under the Copyright Act, no part of this publication may be reproduced, stored in a retrieval system, or transmitted in any form or by any means, electronic, mechanical, photocopying, recording or otherwise, without the prior permission of the publisher. The Catholic Public Domain Version of the Sacred Bible is used unless otherwise stated.

Cataloguing-in-Publication entry is available from the National Library of Australia http://catalogue.nla.gov.au.

This edition first published in 2019
Typesetting by John Healy
Photographs by Julie Mitchell, PhD, are used with permission.

marlene.marburg@kardia.com.au
www.kardia.com.au
marlene@marlenemarburg.com.au
www.marlenemarburg.com.au
PO Box 6024 Doncaster, Victoria 3108 Australia

CONTENTS

Preface. 11

PREPARATION DAYS 15
    Opening words for the retreatant 17
    Spiritual direction 17
    The word 'God' is a metaphor 17
    Communion 18
    God in all things and God in one thing 18
    God's presence 18
    Is God in death, destruction and distortions of love? 18
    Music 20
    Prayer 20
    Desire 21

    Preparation One 23
        Prayer for your spiritual desires 23
        Music 23
        Prayer journal 23
        Examen 24
        Prayer focus for the days of the week 24
        Spiritual direction 25

    Preparation Two 26
        Prayer for your spiritual desires 26
        Examen 26
        Music 26
        Preparation for prayer 26
        Prayer focus for the days of the week 28

    Preparation Three 31
        Prayer for your spiritual desires 31
        Music 31
        Prayer focus for the days of the week 31

    Preparation Four 35
        Prayer for your spiritual desires 35
        Examen 35
        Music 35
        Prayer focus for the days of the week 35

SEASON ONE: LOVE . . . 39
Introduction . . . 41
Movement . . . 41
Choosing where to pray . . . 41
Pattern of prayer . . . 41
Examen . . . 42
The focus of Season One . . . 43
Music . . . 44

Week One . . . 45
Introduction . . . 45
Prayer for your spiritual desires . . . 45
Music . . . 45
Prayer focus for the days of the week . . . 45

Week Two . . . 49
Prayer for your spiritual desires . . . 49
Music . . . 49
Prayer focus for the days of the week . . . 49

Week Three . . . 55
Discernment of your interior movements . . . 55
Prayer for your spiritual desires . . . 55
Music . . . 55
Prayer focus for the days of the week . . . 55

SEASON TWO: INTIMACY . . . 59
Introduction . . . 61
Poetry . . . 61
Music . . . 61
Consolation and Desolation . . . 61
Discernment . . . 62
Writing your own poem . . . 63
Imaginative gospel contemplation . . . 64
Visiting your spiritual director . . . 64
Beginning your prayer of Season Two . . . 65
Savouring prayer . . . 65

Week One . . . 66
Prayer for your spiritual desires . . . 66
Communion of the faithful . . . 66
Journal . . . 66

- Music 66
- Prayer focus for the days of the week. 67
- Music 69

Week Two 71
- Prayer for your spiritual desires. 71
- Journal. 71
- Application of the senses 71
- Imaginative contemplation 72
- At the end of your prayer: a reminder 72
- Music 72
- Body 72
- Prayer focus for the days of the week. 72

Week Three 76
- Praying for the grace. 76
- Music 77
- Body 77
- Prayer focus for the days of the week. 77

Week Four 79
- Preparation for prayer 79
- Prayer for your spiritual desires. 79
- Music 79
- Prayer focus for the days of the week. 79

Week Five 81
- Introduction 81
- Preparation for prayer 81
- Prayer for your spiritual desires. 81
- Music 81
- Prayer focus for the days of the week. 83

Week Six. 87
- Prayer for your spiritual desires. 87
- Music 87
- Prayer focus for the days of the week. 87

Week Seven 90
- Prayer for your spiritual desires. 90
- Music 90
- Prayer focus for the days of the week. 90

Week Eight 93
    Prayer for your spiritual desires. 93
    Music 93
    Prayer focus for the days of the week. 93

Week Nine 96
    Prayer for your spiritual desires. 96
    Music 96
    Prayer focus for the days of the week. 96

Week Ten 100
    Prayer for your spiritual desires. 100
    Music 100
    Prayer focus for the days of the week. 100

Week Eleven 102
    Prayer for your spiritual desires. 102
    Music 102
    Prayer focus for the days of the week. 102

Week Twelve 105
    Prayer for your spiritual desires. 105
    Music 105
    Prayer focus for the days of the week. 105

SEASON THREE: COMPASSION. 107

    Introduction 109
    About your weekly visits to your spiritual director 111
    Music 111

Week One 112
    Prayer for your spiritual desires. 112
    Music 112
    Prayer focus for the days of the week. 113

Week Two 115
    Prayer for your spiritual desires. 115
    Music 115
    Prayer focus for the days of the week. 115

Week Three 118
    Prayer for your spiritual desires. 118
    Music 118
    Prayer focus for the days of the week. 118

Week Four 121
    Prayer for your spiritual desires. 121
    Music 121

Week Five 124
    Prayer for your spiritual desires. 124
    Prayer focus for the days of the week. 124

Week Six 127

SEASON FOUR: JOYFUL PASSION 129

    Introduction 131
    About joy 132
    Music 132
    Contemplatio 132
    Suscipe. 133
    An English version of the Spanish **Suscipe** prayer of Ignatius 134

Week One 135
    Prayer for your spiritual desires. 135
    Music 135
    Prayer focus for the days of the week. 135

Week Two 139
    Prayer for your spiritual desires. 139
    Music 139
    Prayer focus for the days of the week. 139

Week Three 142
    Prayer for your spiritual desires. 142
    Music 142
    Prayer focus for the days of the week. 142

Week Four 144
    Prayer for your spiritual desires. 144
    Music 144
    Prayer focus for the days of the week. 144
    Other possible scriptures 145

Week Five 146
    Prayer for your spiritual desires. 146
    Music 146
    Prayer focus for the days of the week. 147

There is No End to Grace 148
    Preparation Days 148
    Season One: Love 148
    Season Two: Intimacy 149
    Season Three: Compassion 149
    Season Four: Joyful Passion 150
    General Questions 150

Additional material 151
    Preparation Days 151
    Season One: Love 154
    Season Two: Intimacy 157
    Season Three: Compassion 165
    Season Four: Joyful Passion 169

Glossary 171

EIGHT-DAY RETREAT 179
    Opening words for the retreatant 181
    The word 'God' is a metaphor 181
    Communion 181
    God in all things and God in one thing 182
    God's presence 182
    Is God in death, destruction and distortions of Love? 182
    Music 183
    Prayer 184
    Desire 184
    Day One 186
    Imaginative contemplation 186
    Prayer for your spiritual desires 186
    Music 187
    Prayer journal 187
    Examen 187
    Prayer focus for today 187
    Spiritual direction 188
    Day Two 189
    Prayer for your spiritual desires 189
    Examen 189
    Music 189
    Preparation for prayer 189
    Prayer focus for today 190

    Day Three 193
    Principle and Foundation 193
    Prayer for your spiritual desires. 194
    Music 194
    Prayer focus for today 194
    Day Four. 197
    Prayer for your spiritual desires. 197
    Examen 197
    Music 197
    Prayer focus for today 197
    Day Five 200
    Introduction 200
    Prayer for your spiritual desires. 200
    Music 200
    Prayer focus for today 200
    Day Six. 203
    Prayer for your spiritual desires. 203
    Music 203
    Prayer focus for today 203
    Day Seven 207
    Discernment of your interior movements 207
    Prayer for your spiritual desires. 207
    Music 207
    Prayer focus for today 207
    Day Eight 210
    Prayer for your spiritual desires. 210
    Music 210

Post Day Eight 216

Bibliography 218

Acknowledgements 220

Love is the most universal, the most tremendous and the most mystical of cosmic forces. Love is the primal and universal psychic energy. Love is a sacred reserve of energy; it is like the blood of spiritual evolution.

Pierre Teilhard de Chardin SJ
(The Spirit of the Earth, 1931. IV, 32, 33 and 34)

Preface

Grace upon Grace: Savouring the Spiritual Exercises through the Arts is an inclusive and contemporary retreat to be prayed daily for 30 weeks. This retreat has the same dynamic seasons as that of the *Spiritual Exercises of Saint Ignatius of Loyola* written in the early sixteenth century. *Grace upon Grace* is necessarily an adaptation of Ignatius' *Spiritual Exercises* for the 21st century.

Ignatius' *Spiritual Exercises* invite a person into an ongoing experience of freedom, releasing spiritual gifts of enlightenment and empowerment. In *Grace upon Grace*, freedom is understood as an ongoing release from spiritual ignorance and psychological entrapment in destructive thought patterns and behaviour. Freedom is co-creativity with Mystery known by many names, such as God, Source, Love or Presence. Mystery is not restricted by concepts or retreat processes, but calls us to participate fully in the creativity that brought us into being in the first place. The spirit of *Grace upon Grace: Savouring the Spiritual Exercises through the Arts*, like that of the sixteenth century *Spiritual Exercises of Saint Ignatius,* makes real the calling of God on human life, and fosters attentiveness to the future which is already budding within us.

A person who prays this retreat can expect to be invited into full engagement and integration of their whole self in relationship with Mystery. The retreat supports creative expression of that relationship. The specific graces of each 'season' may be experienced by anyone opening themselves to God, in all things, and the sacred connection between all things.

The book reflects the poetic nature of the Christian scriptures, particularly the gospels, thus extending their relevance beyond the usual Christian audience to anyone who wants to participate in living their authentic humanity fully and freely. While using the Judeo-Christian scriptures, the theology underpinning these spiritual exercises refutes any claims to elitism and the ultimate truth of any religious system. This refutation at the same time affirms that there are multiple interpretations of the content of any belief system. At best, theology only ever points to God. Thus this retreat is offered to all women and men, and attempts to remove all presuppositions of patriarchy and gender inequality.

In 2013, I finished my PhD entitled *Poetry and Grace: Exploring Poetry as Prayer in the Context of Ignatian Spirituality*. I expected subsequently to write a book on the Ignatian exercises. I did not expect, however, that I would be propelled on a journey which made every attempt to write such a book somewhat unsatisfying. Gradually I was taken on an enlarging journey where science and spirituality became not only compatible but completed interrelated. Increasingly, we encounter spiritual persons who experience shared ground with a consciousness of deeper, wordless realities, regardless of their spiritual traditions. The practice of spiritual direction, with its strong roots in Christianity, is increasingly finding methods and content aligned with disciplines such as process-oriented psychology, arts-based therapies and quantum consciousness. Bibliotherapy and poetry therapy also, with their emphasis on story and metaphor can contribute positively to spirituality and the experience of spiritual direction. These disciplines offer word-languages expansive enough to point to the Mystery of God.

So there is poetry in this book, and many other offerings from the arts to help a retreatant to become centred and prayerful. Thirty or more pieces of Music are suggested to support the experience and dynamic of the 'seasons'. Movement and dance are invited. Ways of praying, mandalas and poetry are explained and encouraged. A Glossary is provided. You will find additional poetry at the end of the retreat material. All these artistic expressions are placed at the service of the retreatant seeking authentic freedom in God.

In this book, both consolation and desolation, explained in the Glossary, are understood as opportunities to grow in grace. The daily Examen, imaginative contemplation, contemporary versions of the Principle and Foundation, the *Suscipe* and Ignatian meditations are included. These terms are also explained in the Glossary. There is opportunity to ponder personal stories, dreams and desires, as well as obstacles to personal freedom. It is suggested that the experience of the person who prays this retreat will be enhanced by the companionship and guidance of a weekly conversation with an Ignatian spiritual director.

Near the end of the book, a second, shorter retreat is offered: Grace upon Grace, an eight-day retreat. This retreat has been developed to address issues related to gendered language and images of God that may have become obsolete in the minds of many retreatants.

Preface

In writing this book, I have not only read and engaged the *Spiritual Exercises* again and again, but I have deepened my awareness of the consoling grace that is continuously available in God.

Grace upon Grace respects the Christian history on which it is built. The book embraces contemporary spiritualities, contemporary scientific exploration into the origin and unity of life, and the spaciousness of poetic language and the arts. In order to undertake these exercises, you will need a Christian Bible, preferably a translation rather than a paraphrase. You will also need at least one journal to honour your thoughts and feelings. Your journal will become another text to receive and savour truth and grace.

I trust you will find freedom in God through these exercises.

Marlene Marburg

Preparation Days

I have stilled and quieted my soul;
… Like a weaned child is my soul within me.
(Psalm 131:2. ASV)[1]

---

[1] *American Standard Version* of the Bible.

Opening words for the retreatant

Welcome to the retreat in everyday life: *Grace upon Grace: Savouring the Spiritual Exercises through the Arts*. The book is presented as a series of spiritual exercises to be followed daily. You will have your own reasons for wanting to pray these exercises. Ignatius of Loyola[1] who wrote the original *Spiritual Exercises*[2] expressed their value and intention when he said that they were exercises to free a person (*'soul'*) from **disabling tendencies**[3] **in order to live fully in loving communion with God, and hence act from that abundant love [1].**[4]

Spiritual direction

If you can find a **spiritual director** to accompany you through the Exercises, you will be able to share and discuss anything which is important to you. While some spiritual directors, who are also givers of the Exercises, confine the conversation to what has happened in your **prayer**, it is important to find a director who will also welcome conversation about what is happening in your life. You and your spiritual director together will seek to know the direction to which God is drawing you.

The word 'God' is a metaphor

In this book, the metaphor for the **Mystery** of life or the dynamic Sustainer of all things is 'God'. While my **desire** is to be fully inclusive, certain words, including 'God', can jar on our sensibilities for reasons that are unique to each of us. If it is helpful, discuss with your spiritual director any word that

---

1 Tylenda, *A Pilgrim's Journey: The Autobiography of St. Ignatius Loyola*. This text is an example of one autobiography available.
2 Fleming, *Draw Me into Your Friendship* is the version of the *Spiritual Exercises* used in this book.
3 Consult the Glossary for words which are bolded and italicised when used for the first time in this book.
4 *The Spiritual Exercises of Saint Ignatius* are divided into numerated paragraphs [Annotations 1–20], Spiritual Exercises [21] Presupposition [22] Principle and Foundation [23] and Notations [24 and following]. They denote the generally accepted paragraphs in any of Elder Mullan's translations of the Spanish Autograph version of Ignatius' *Spiritual Exercises*. In the present text, such numbers are enclosed in square brackets.

jars, replacing it with what seems helpful to you. If you are unsure of the intended meaning of any word in bold type, consult the Glossary near the end of the book.

Communion

If God is the sustainer of all things, God is in communion with us and all of God's creation. Communion is the movement to which we are called, and in openness, we find ourselves drawn into God. When disruption and chaos inevitably come into our lives, God invites us to listen at ever deepening levels.[5]

God in all things and God in one thing

There are two (or more) connected premises on which *Grace upon Grace: Savouring the Spiritual Exercises through the Arts* is built: firstly, as in the *Spiritual Exercises of Saint Ignatius of Loyola*, God is understood as present and able to be experienced in all things. Secondly, all seemingly separate things are understood as contributing to a unified whole.

God's presence

We do not have to beg God to be with us. God is already participating in the cosmic, universal and particular aspects of life. God-within-us has the potential to enable the fulfilment of an intimate and infinite journey into the reality of God. Our physical senses sometimes deceive us into thinking that the world we perceive is all there is. We are easily distracted from a deeper knowing that God is the source of all we are.

Our spiritual senses help us to believe and trust that God might desire us, just as we desire God. As we lean into this hope, we share in the experience of people from many streams of spirituality who know that as we open ourselves to God, we find God waiting in *love*. It seems that our deeper desires are awakened and inflamed by God's desires. If we allow space for God to be who or what God wants to be in us, we find God already present. We forget our *ego*-selves and become one with God and all things.

Is God in death, destruction and distortions of love?

While the word 'God' and the nature of 'God' might be problematic for

---

[5] [6] Rohr, *When Things Fall Apart*. Email linked to online daily meditations.

some, the idea that God is in all things, including destructive behaviour, is likely to be problematic for many. God, whom many refer to as Love, seems to be at odds with destruction. How can God be Love and be in all things? How can God be in destruction, death, suffering, disaster and violence? Perhaps the complexity of this question can be explored a little by the following faith statements:

God is always present. God is present in our human ability and in our power to create and destroy. But God never desires the diminution of love. It seems that God prevents neither love nor hate, but is a resistant force in the hearts of those who are victims of violence. When people behave destructively, they diminish themselves; evil punishes evil. Destruction is apparently part of the ongoing cycle of life, just as we see in nature when a star, for example, becomes depleted of nuclear fuel, and explodes. To this point in time, cosmic life has emerged as a power which is more creative than it is destructive. On earth, God's **grace** or energy continues to bring about new abundance and life-giving **transformation**. Actions such as love, compassion and benevolence contribute to this abundance that God animates minute by minute. God is present even in distortions of creativity, such as when humans misappropriate or abuse God's creative powers. Due to such misuse of power, the pathway to human transformation becomes more circuitous and takes longer for both the perpetrator and those whom the perpetrator affects.

Distortion and destruction are not the same thing, and God is present in both. What we perceive as destruction, such as death, is part of the natural cycle of life, death and new life (***resurrection***). While destruction appears to be the breaking down of created things, it is not their obliteration. Is anything ever totally destroyed? It appears that resurrection or transformation (of energy from one form to another) eventually emerges through the apparent chaos of creativity, destruction and the distortion of creative power.

> The conservation of energy is an absolute law, and yet it seems to fly in the face of things we observe every day. Sparks create a fire, which generates heat—manifest energy that wasn't there before. A battery produces power. A nuclear bomb creates an explosion. Each of these situations, however, is simply a case of energy

changing form.[6]

None of us has the whole picture of why we have the **freedom** to use and abuse God's creativity in us. While physics, cosmology and the theology of free will are helpful in opening us to the expansiveness of God, they are incomplete forms of knowledge. In addition, these sciences and the explanations they offer are not the primary focus of this retreat. God, and the creative consciousness of your relationship with God, is the focus.

Notice what brings life to you and what takes it from you – this is a key to your evolving *self* in life and during your days of the spiritual exercises.

Music

Music is selected to support you in this retreat, but as affinity with music depends on personal taste, I encourage you to choose music which will support you at the various stages of the retreat.

- Music: Ólafur Arnalds *Þú ert jörðin* (You are the earth) on the album *Living Room Songs*. 2011.

Prayer

Prayer is primarily awareness of God; it is being with God and acting with God. Your whole life can be prayer. Your presence on this planet earth makes clear that God desires for you to exist. You have already been brought into being by God. God is within you. You are able to be in the river of God's desire.

As you pray this retreat asking for the grace to deepen your awareness of God in your life, know that you are joining with spiritual seekers around the globe from many traditions, or from no tradition at all.

The exercises in *Grace upon Grace: Savouring the Spiritual Exercises through the Arts* contain poetry, images and music references, as well as excerpts from texts, especially the Judeo-Christian scriptures. Poetry is the language of the soul. It is open and spacious and allows a person to enter the words with their own story, drawing meaning in ways that frequently transcend rational thought.

Although the exercises are not prescriptive, they are chosen to take you

---

6 Moskowitz, 'Fact or fiction: Energy can neither be created nor destroyed', *Scientific American*, online.

through the dynamics and graces of the retreat in ways that are compatible with everyday life. These exercises move through **seasons**; each season having its particular characteristics. In life we have seasons of abundant energy, intrigue, grief, loss and sometimes of heartfelt celebration. The four seasons presented in the pages that follow are preceded by a preparation period, comprising four weeks of prayer. These weeks lay a strong foundation for the four seasons which follow. You and your spiritual director might discern that more time is needed for the preparation period; it is helpful to move through the retreat at the pace that is right for you.

Your desire to draw more closely to God in your life is the main element of prayer. You will also need time each day to dedicate to prayer. Your spiritual director guiding this retreat will listen to you, respond to your sharing and hold the process through the 30 or so weeks of the retreat. If you are praying this retreat in 30 days, your spiritual director will easily adapt the prayer material for you. One week's prayer in daily life is equivalent to one day's prayer in a silent, enclosed 30-day retreat. It is anticipated that during the 30-week retreat, a person will pray for one hour each day, plus 10–15 minutes at some point in the day or evening, to pray the **Examen** prayer.

Desire

In this retreat, you will be asked to pray for what you desire. What does it mean to pray for what you desire? Desires are not superficial 'wants'; they are deeply felt aspects of love. The prayer of desire might be the prayer not to desire something, not to long for love or beauty, not to want to change or manipulate anything. Sometimes we desire God intensely but have not yet realized that we are already inextricably united with God. Sometimes our longing is to experience feelings that we associate with God – peace, joy, love. Desiring God is not about feeling good or bad. It is about relinquishing personal wants in favour of what God desires for us at that particular time. Sometimes our desire might be simply to have no desire, or to pray a prayer of presence, or simply to 'show up' for prayer, however in these instances prayer is nevertheless intentional, however small that intention is.

We are body, mind and spirit people. Although we speak of these three aspects, they form one entity. An authentic desire will never be irrational to you, although it might be non-rational or beyond rational. When we pray in accordance with our deepest desires, we are actually moving along the prayerful journey in union with God. The 'Take and Receive' prayer expressed Ignatius' desire:

> **Take and Receive**
>
> Take, ... [God], and receive all my liberty, my memory, my understanding, and my entire will, all that I have and call my own. You have given it all to me. To you ... I return it. Everything is yours; Do with it what you will. Give me only your love and your grace. That is enough for me [234].[7]

In this retreat, desires are not tangible, not material. They are spiritual. Prayer for your spiritual desires is a reminder to live consciously in the flow of God's grace. It asks you to pay attention to what is happening in your life and what life is asking of you.

So to the ever-present God we turn, as we engage in the following exercises.

---

[7] Fleming, *Draw Me into Your Friendship,* p. 177. This is Fleming's paraphrase of Ignatius' *Suscipe* prayer.

Preparation One

Prayer for your spiritual desires

This week you are invited to the prayer of **imaginative contemplation**. This kind of contemplation honours your capacity to be present to the events in stories you read, especially those in the gospels. Your imagination takes you into the story and leads you on a journey of discovery about yourself and how you respond to and experience different people, circumstances and events.

So, what is your *desire* as you begin? You could seek to be found by God. You could ask to know God's love for you. You could desire to know God more fully. You could wonder about how God is with you. You could pray to know and be the person God imagined and created you to be. Could you pray to know more deeply your oneness with God?

If you dare

to put your heart in there
it will catch fire
and when hearts are aflame
there is assurance

no more daring

just sparks of the dream
showering stardust
awakening

Music
- Lisa Kelly, 'May It Be' on the album *Celtic Woman Presents: Lisa*. 2006.

Prayer journal

There are many books which claim that writing is a transformative tool or a pathway to awakening. Your **prayer journal** is usually a written record of your prayer each day, especially the ways in which you were moved interiorly during your prayer. Some people choose to represent their experience in art or poetry. Some choose movement and dance.

Examen

For 10–15 minutes at the end of each day, notice your desire. Are you moving towards your desire, or is anything moving you away?

Prayer focus for the days of the week

1. Psalm 131. My soul is like a weaned child that is within me. Imagine yourself with Mother God and the weaned child. What is it like being present to these events?
2. Luke 15:1–7. Parable about God's mercy and love: the lost sheep is found. Refer to the Glossary for the meaning of 'imaginative contemplation'. Allow your imagination to lead you through this gospel story.
3. Luke 15:1–3; 8–10. Parable about the lost coin which is found. Today, ponder any meanings you can find in this parable.

Find me

In the nocturnal enclosure, sparse
shadows and child-voice rise, calling, <i>Dark!</i>
Find me!

4. Luke 15:1–3; 11–32. Parable about God's mercy and love: the lost son, who returns to himself and his family.
5. Read the poem 'Prodigal love' below. Choose a line or two to ponder. You could also choose from other poems, such as 'Prodigal sequence' which you will find in the additional material at the end of the retreat. 'Prodigal sequence' is an imaginative contemplation on the imagined family of the lost son in Luke 15.

Prodigal love

The trees do not breathe
at the end of this weary August day.
Flat, leaden air surrounds me.
My temples ache

as I recuperate from yesterday
thinking

of the prodigal mystery
whose eyes lay a satin cloak
over my unwashed shame.

I am unsure of myself –

I know what is under the cloak,
the tainted hands
on which the ring is placed

but I feel pain and the spill of tears,
my father's anointing.

6. **Savouring prayer.** When praying a '*savouring prayer*', pray over a poignant moment from a previous day's prayer: Which words, feelings or ideas in a previous prayer struck you today as meaningful? Return to yesterday's prayer; did any part of that prayer bring a new or deeper awareness of God's desire for you?

7. **Examen of the week.** Conscious of God's presence, ponder the experiences from your week of prayer. You might begin to notice what thoughts prompted experiences of love and what thoughts threatened love. What might be God's invitation to you? Have the desires and graces for which you are praying changed in some way?

Spiritual direction

At your meetings with your spiritual director, share your experiences of prayer and how prayer and life interact. Sometimes you will find that your prayer experiences deepen during ***spiritual direction.***

Preparation Two

Prayer for your spiritual desires

What do you want? What is your deepening desire as you begin this second week of prayer? You could pray as you did last week, to know God more fully. You could pray to experience the love God has for you. You could pray to see yourself as God sees you. You could pray to be the person God imagined and created you to be. Could you pray to be one with God?

> *Your God is the strength in your midst. [God] will save ... will rejoice over you with gladness. In love, [God] will be silent. [And God] will exalt over you with praise* (Zephaniah 3:17).
>
> *Your voice is sweet and your face is graceful* (Song of Songs 2:16 CPDV; other versions 2:14).[1]

Examen

At a regular time each day, take 10–15 minutes to remember

- the most important graced experience of the day, and
- the experience which brought the greatest challenges.

Can you hear God's loving invitation in these things? What is emerging for you?

Music

- Ray LaMontagne (singer-songwriter), 'Be Here Now' on the album Till the Sun Turns Black. Produced by Ethan Johns. Advance Music. 2006.

Preparation for prayer

Using the poetic image 'Prepositioning God' as your preparation for each day's prayer this week, gaze on the page (with your eyes half shut if it helps) initially discounting the words, until you rest on a page position which

---

[1] The Catholic Public Domain Version (CPDV) of the Bible is the text used in this book unless otherwise stated. Note that chapter and verse numbers in the CPDV differ slightly from other versions.

attracts you. You do not have to know why. Stay with that position on the page. Check the word that is closest to your chosen position. Does that word speak to you about your relationship with God at present? If not, what word might better express your position with God?

Prepositioning God

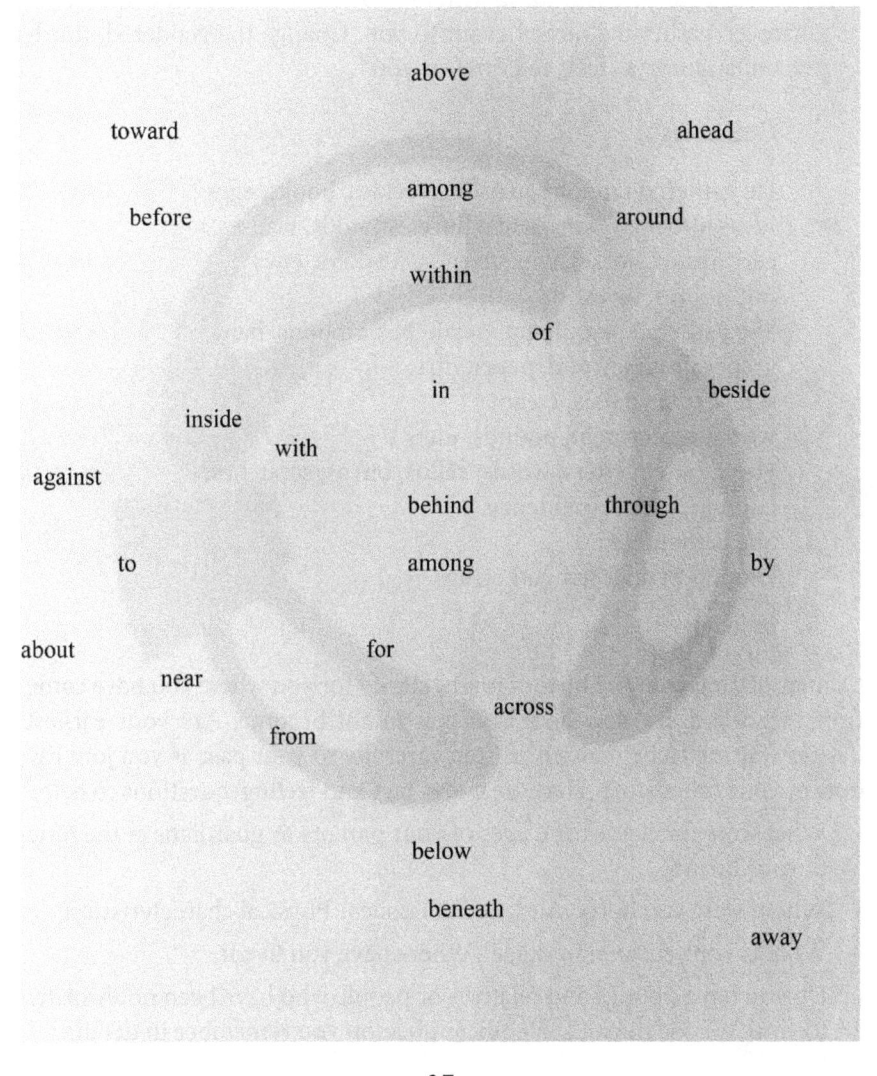

above

toward   ahead

among

before   around

within

of

inside   in   beside

with

against

behind   through

to   among   by

about   for

near

across

from

below

beneath

away

Prayer focus for the days of the week

1. Hosea 11:1–8. *I will draw them ... with bands of love.*
2. Luke 4:16–30. *The spirit of the Lord is upon me.* Imaginative contemplation.
3. Psalm 139. God knew you before you were born. What part of this psalm resonates with your desires?
4. Pray over your life, beginning with the poem 'Gatherers'. Add and delete whatever 'gatherings' are relevant to you. Change the gendered, third-person language as feels relevant for you.

Gatherers

He gathered tadpoles, daisies, freckles, books, eggs,
ideas, dreams, plans, fears, hurts, shoulds, bruises,
certificates, possessions, friends, feathers, envy
joy, desires, loves.
She gathered pegs, nappies, stitches, ribbons, hair,
grapes, leaves, wood, paper, dirt,
skirts, tulle, petals, cream
worry, resentment, pounds, diets.
He gathered letters, words, callus, burns, scratches,
courage, grief, confidence.
She gathered trust
enough to offer her gatherings

to let go.

Contemplating your life history might clarify for you where you have come from, who you are now and who you might become. Are your earliest desires waiting to be realised? Listen carefully to your past as you join the dots of your fuller story. Here are a few 'fact and feeling' questions to help:

- What were the names and ages of your parents or guardians at the time of your birth?
- Where were you born? Any medical issues? Physical characteristics?
- What is your cultural heritage? Where have you lived?
- Do you have siblings and relatives or people who have been noteworthy to you? Who is the most significant person you remember in detail?

Preparation Days

- For what are you thankful? For what is it difficult for you to be thankful?

  > Come, come, whoever you are. Wanderer, worshipper, lover of leaving. It doesn't matter. Ours is not a caravan of despair. Come, even if you have broken your vows a thousand times. Come, yet again, come, come. [2]
  >
  > .... *Jelaluddin Rumi* [3]

- List some traits or characteristics you have possibly developed as a result of your environment, your family and life circumstances. Note also the traits or characteristics which seem to have a genetic basis.
- List what you like and dislike about yourself. Spend more time on what you like, noting how well these attributes have served you.
- What role has God has played in all these things? How do you feel towards God in relation to these things?
- Note some characteristics in yourself that you don't like. Stay with this, honouring the history of your experience. Do you want a conversation with God about this? What does God say about you?
- In your *journal*, record your *interior movements* about these reflections on your life.

5. Psalm 139. Savour a prayer from a previous day's **contemplation**.
6. Principle and Foundation of the *Spiritual Exercises* [23], paraphrase one, written in the first person:

   > I am created to be who God wants to be in me. I am intended to bring beauty and fullness to all that God creates and empowers me to be and do. God imagined me out of love, for love. Only in love can God's full imagination be realised. Only in full communion with God can all persons and all reality know and experience wholeness.
   >
   > God's world has undergone change through conscious and unconscious human action, some which seems disordered. Disorder is not flux or the polarities of

---
[2] Rumi. Goodreads. 'Quotes: Quotable quotes'.
[3] Goodreads. 'Rumi'. Rumi was a 13th century Persian poet who lived in Konya in present-day Turkey.

everyday life but the failure to recognise and act in accordance with the love of God instilled in our hearts. This love inspires me to participate in my life-world through my personal authentic gifts. It enables me to find from the choices available to me that which will empower or disempower my life. What reason would I have to choose disempowerment? Why would I ever choose to disconnect myself from my life source?

7. Savour your experiences of God in your week of prayer or deepen a prayer from one of the days of the week.

Preparation Three

Prayer for your spiritual desires

What is your desire as you begin this week of prayer? You could pray to be open. You could pray, as in previous weeks, to know God more fully. You could pray to know the love God has for you. You could pray to see yourself as God sees you. You could pray to be the person God imagined and created you to be, that is, the person you really are.

Before your prayer, breathe in God's life-giving energy. Pay attention to how your body feels, giving special attention and care to the weaker parts. Then you might pray this prophetic text each day:

> *I will give them an undivided heart and put a new spirit in them; I will remove from them their heart of stone and give them a heart of flesh* (Ezekiel 11:19).

Remember to pray the Examen each day.[1]

Music

- Audrey Assad, 'O My Soul' on the album Audrey Assad: Heart, produced by Marshall Altman et al. 2012.

Prayer focus for the days of the week

1. Isaiah 45:7–13. I form light and create darkness.

   Vessels are hollow

   Wedged and thrown, the ball of clay
   spins, plays in liquid hands.
   Mastery of thumbs and fingers
   persuade perfect balance, symmetry,
   a rearrangement of raw earth
   rising against resistant forces,
   forming a hollow the clay anticipates, desires.

---

[1] A helpful and simple book on the Examen, for both adults and children, is: D Linn, S.F. Linn and M. Linn, *Sleeping with Bread: Holding What Gives You Life,* 1995.

Its character awaits this test, this moment,
every moment.

The potter senses through clay-skin and
cracked and muscled hands, through
terracotta under fingernails,
a thrilling, urgent shaping,
an accelerating wheel, a dizzy race.

But she dreams:
molten clay
explosions in the kiln
sentinels on pedestals
warnings
and finally, a settled fearless voice
heard beneath it all.

Daybreak verge,
she bypasses the wheel,
stands before studio shelves,
selects a crazed, wide-mouthed raku pot;
an ornament, hand-built, fired once.
She smiles
at each face in turn,
listens to each line and incline speak.

She prepares a generous glaze,
patient green in its hollow.

A second firing, risking, cooling.

Slowly she runs her finger-tips
over the rough and tepid surface,

raises the pot to the light,
examines its interior for cracks, flaws.

She smells the pot,
takes breath from its hollow.

She speaks into it
and from it –
an ornament no more,
a ready vessel.

2. Recall your earliest dream or memory. Recalling the earliest dream or memory, especially the energy in the characters, can be transformative. If the dream or memory is disturbing, are you able to share it with your spiritual director, who will help you talk about it? If the energy feels strong and fearful, consider how that energy might be transformed. If you are not ready for this prayer, put it aside for a later time. (There is no right or wrong about your decision.) Below is a process for praying about a dream:
   - Remember you are in God's presence. Recall your earliest childhood dream or your earliest memory. In your journal, write as many details as you can, noting what happened, where it happened, who the characters were, what they were doing, how they behaved, what was their appearance, how you felt towards the characters in the dream, and how they were towards you.

   This earliest childhood dream or memory is thought to have significance for your whole life journey, although once you are conscious of this dream or memory, it does not have to dictate the way your life will be. For Jung, first dreams are archetypal. They come from the wisdom of the collective unconscious. Your earliest remembered dream has energy in it, sometimes fearful and sometimes pleasant.
   - Imagine ways in which the ***dreambody*** can use energy in a positive way. Have a conversation with God about these memories, receiving God's invitation to transform the dream energy into useful energies for your life.

   You might find that the energy of the figure you fear in the dream is the energy you need to be creative. This energy is already in you. Do you believe that the future is already taking shape in you?
3. Ephesians 2:1–10. Am I living the life to which God has called me?
4. Principle and Foundation of the *Spiritual Exercises* [23], paraphrase two:

   God desires us and draws us closely. We experience God's desire as a heart-felt knowing and desire to be immersed in and unified with the life of God we encounter in our life-world. As we participate in God's grace, we find we are drawn by an ever-increasing desire to respond to God's personal call on our lives. To discern that call in the large and smaller choices available to us, we endeavour to stand neutrally before them, committing the decisions to God. We are able to do this because many of our desires are subordinate to the deepest call and desire with which God has gifted us – to love God, learn more of the way of **Christ** in us and communicate the love of Christ to others.

5. Romans 8:28. In what way have all things worked together for good in your life? How might you understand 'good'?
6. Savouring day. Pray today about anything which has emerged as dark, distasteful, bland or problematic during these last days. On the other hand, you might pray pondering and savouring anything which has drawn you towards light and love.
7. Romans 7:14–25. God has chosen love to defeat the powers that would thwart potential.
8. John 1:1–18. In the beginning …

Preparation Four

Prayer for your spiritual desires

You are nearing the end of the preparation days. For what grace would you like to pray this week?

What is your disposition towards God; how are you with God? Has your image of God changed in any way over these weeks of prayer? Are you choosing freely to pray the spiritual exercises? Does this seem to be God's desire for you?

During each prayer period of Preparation Four, recall a favourite passage of scripture or a line or two of a poem or song which helps you to picture God in relationship with you. As a preparation for prayer, repeat your chosen words as a way of savouring your experience of God with you.

Examen

Each day this week when praying the Examen, think about what might help you to flourish and experience yourself as a loving person. Are there any barriers to your freedom to receive and give love?

Music

- Audrey Assad, 'You Speak' on the album Fortunate Fall, produced by Audrey Assad on Fortunate Fall Records. 2013.

Prayer focus for the days of the week

Isaiah 54:4–10. *For the mountains will be moved, and the hills will tremble. But my mercy will not depart from you.*

1. Psalm 91. God protects and cares for you.
2. Pray the prayer-poem 'God'.

   God

   You speak to me,
   You are close.
   I hear as words from my deepest self.

From here I am to be healed,
replenished and consoled.

Let me feel living waters
splash upon my heart.
Drench me in the gift of You.
Lord teach me who I am in You.
Hold me strong
and don't let go
even when I do.

Keep my eyes open
transfixed to you and your eternal desire.

I am certain You will draw me to Yourself,
for You are Love's Self,
Who delights
in the simplest murmurings of praise
which he and she and I together
cannot help but hum.

3. Jeremiah 1:1–19. Jeremiah's call. *You shall go ... to everyone to whom I shall send you.*
4. Poem 'Toe print'.

Toe print

In my first step,
I put my toe-print
on God's rejoicing earth,
and all else I am
stirs in hopeful breath.

As I grow in gripping steps,
I think
my toe-print is my own.
I do not think
where it has come from

or where it is going.
I do not hear
beneath my feet, the praise
of leaves and stones
and puddles, ants and snails,
the tenor of other toe-prints
longing for our God.

And as I grow in faltering steps,
I sense
within each line, each whorl,
a belonging to God's infinite labyrinth
and each step,
a trusting one of many
given just to me.

5. Psalm 131. Return to Psalm 131 to rest on the lap of Mother God.
6. Deuteronomy 1:29–32. God carries you.
7. Exodus 3:1–10. Burning bush. *Here I am.*

Season One: Love

Let there be you.
And it was so.

Season One: Love

Introduction

Grace upon Grace: Savouring the Spiritual Exercises through the Arts is an invitation to a deepening relationship with God. The prayers intentionally invite the engagement of your whole self. Remember that there is no hierarchy in ways of praying. God is in all kinds of prayer. It is said that prayer as poetry or poetry as prayer is one of the purest languages of the human spirit. Poetry is open to interpretation and does not limit God. But there are other pure 'languages' of the spirit, such as movement, art or sound which you are encouraged to use freely as you pray these spiritual exercises.

Movement

Movement can be prayer itself. It amplifies your feelings and expresses your responses to God. It can be a way of self-discovery. Movement may be the simplest stroke of a pencil or a flamboyant dance. The subtlest of movements, such as the heartbeat, pulse or breathing, can be registered as a prayer movement in the seeming stillness.

Choosing where to pray

Your chosen prayer space can complement the content of each day's prayer. You are invited to enter your place of prayer imaginatively as well as practically, choosing an environment which is conducive to prayer for you. As you sit in your prayer space at home, rest on a rock beside the ocean, walk in the bush or forest or your own neighborhood; as you gaze upon a desert landscape or snow-covered mountains, you might experience spontaneously the grace God desires for you.

Pattern of prayer

- Settle into an open disposition before God. Recall a grace from last week which helps you to settle into prayer. Be with God.
- Ask God for the grace you are seeking.
- Read the given text(s) twice. Texts are from a variety of sources.
- Be present to the words touching you. Allow God to 'gaze' into your heart, especially the parts of you that you feel need restoring in some way.

Grace Upon Grace: Savouring the Spiritual Exercises through the Arts

- Ponder for a while.
- Sometimes it is helpful to have a 'conversation' with someone who has come to mind as you pray. This might be a character in the text.
- Have a conversation with God.
- Reflect on the prayer, and name your grace with a thankful heart.
- Give some creative expression to your time with God; journal, write a poem, draw, sing or dance.

Examen

Remember to pray the Examen each evening or at a time suitable to you. Here is a poetic way to pray the Examen prayer:

The olive branch

The first thing: make friends with yourself.
Search your story.
Look at your hands.

Let them take centre stage for a time,
as Marcel Marceau,[1]
silent witness to their wisdom
and charisma.

Find Susan Boyle[2] born
to silence the critic in you.

Applaud yourself.
Watch the gracious bow,
the whole cast
in the production of you.

Hold left and right
hands together as friends,
as strangers, shamed and frail
the child with limping moods,

---

1 French actor and mime artist Marcel Marceau (1923–2007). He performed his silent art for over 60 years.
2 Scottish singer Susan Magdalane Boyle (1961–) was discovered on *Britain's Got Talent* on 11 April 2009, singing 'I Dreamed a Dream' from *Les Misérables*.

the frightened talent,
the sensitive heart,
creator and director,
who know how to cast
all biases aside,

left and right
who cause and know hurt,
who love and long for love.

Restore and love the threads of yourself,
hidden stories your heart touches and must tell,
the dossier and poem-story
you hear in your dreams,
pieced,
stitched and layered in Mystery
joining your hands again.

The focus of Season One

During Season One: Love, you are asked again to contemplate God's desire for you. Imagine God looking at you (Genesis 1:31) and living within you. Although at times you might feel God is absent, how can that be true? God is present in all things, continually imagining and creating and giving birth to all natural life. God is with you in your involuntary breathing and heartbeat. As a child, you might have grown up with an **anthropomorphic** image of God, which helps your understanding of a personal, relational God. In holding such an image, God is also likely to be imaged as a person's parents or carers, and that can be confusing. In Season One, anchor yourself in the scripture which affirms that nothing can '*separate us from the love of God, which is in Christ Jesus*' (see Romans 8:38–39).

As you pray the spiritual exercises, you will notice some of your psychological or religious 'baggage' emerging. Perhaps you have a sense of an impersonal, remote God, or one who doesn't actually care about who you are or what you do. Perhaps you understand the language of 'God' as synonymous with religion. Perhaps 'God' equates in your mind with fundamentalist religious violence and abuse, and their prevalence across the globe.

During Season One, you are asked to ponder good, evil, love and hate in a personal way. How are you participating in the destruction and creativity of your own life and the life of the world? Consider what you see, hear and feel in your body, mind and spirit as your pray, read, listen to the music suggested and follow any of the other steps suggested during Season One. The point of praying through Season One is not to berate or punish yourself but to raise your awareness about patterns of thinking and acting which take life from you and others.

Season One is about God as Love – God's love for us – and how we may consciously or unconsciously diminish or reject it. In Season One of Ignatius' *Spiritual Exercises*, readers are asked to pray for the grace of '**shame** and confusion' [48.4] at having dishonoured themselves while God creates and honours them. In these spiritual exercises, you will be guided to ask for the grace of **humility** in the face of God's unconditional, abundant love for you. You might ask for the grace to notice your own compassionate love or to increase your **self-compassion**.

You might want to share with your spiritual director how you feel when you are *drawn* to particular choices, and how you feel when you are *driven* to particular choices. Explore what it means to be balanced in relation to the choices available to you [23]. Become familiar with your own patterns of thinking, feeling and behaving. These are the checkpoints for discernment.

Music

Alexandre Desplat, 'Light and Darkness' on the album *Tree of Life* motion picture album. AllMusic. 2011.

Week One

Introduction

During this first week of Season One: Love, you are invited to ask God to enlighten you to the many ways that evil, disguised as 'good', might have a hold on organisations, relationships and individuals. Ask to be shown the way in which human actions impact others, the earth with whom we have a delicate relationship, and the whole cosmos which we are affecting even in minute ways. How might God view these events and experiences, and in turn, how do you view them?

Prayer for your spiritual desires

This week, pray for the grace to hear God's personal invitation of love to you. You might ask, as Ignatius does, for the grace of 'shame and confusion' [48.4] at having dishonoured yourself while God continues to create and honour you. You could ask for the grace of humility in the face of God's unconditional, abundant love. You might ask for the grace to notice your own compassionate love or to increase your self-compassion.

Music

- Steffany Gretzinger, 'No Fear in Love' on the album *The Undoing*. Music and lyrics: Bethel. 2014.

Prayer focus for the days of the week

1. Recall a documentary film, a movie, or a newspaper item which speaks to the way in which greed or ego-driven-ness is depicted in an organisation or a person. Take some time over this. Read Luke 10:18–20. Read the scriptures as poetry, and the poetry below as scripture.

    Waiting for Love

    God, You are an unrequited lover,
    lovesick for me,
    waiting for the smallest hope,
    even a glance of recognition.

You are always in love,
waiting for me to fall in love.

2. Try the pattern of prayer given in the introduction to Season One. Pray for the grace to be present to God's love. Today's prayer focuses on the way we develop and assert our point of view. You might pray to be at balance with all things. How have you developed patterns of acceptance and criticism? Notice where you are critical of others but lenient on yourself. Notice where you are critical of yourself and lenient on others. Become aware of ways you might have knowingly and unknowingly contributed to the diminishment of life and love.

> In the context of a political justice issue which brings into focus matters of race, gender, sexuality and difference, how do you respond to the following report from 2016? This article is a suggestion for contemplation. You might find a similar article in current media.

During the 2015 election, a briefing written by the London School of Economics' Centre for Economic Performance showed: There is still no evidence of an overall negative impact of immigration on jobs, wages, housing or the crowding out of public services … One of the largest impacts of immigration seems to be on public perceptions.[1]

3. Genesis 3:1–19. The narrative of the man and the woman in the garden [51]. The man and the woman are everyman and everywoman. Focus on God as you recall your story in the likeness of 'Adam' or 'Eve'.

4. Luke 12:20. The focus of prayer today is personal *sin* [55]. Pray for the grace to be open to notice your responses to temptations and your patterns of thought which are not life-giving. Pray for the grace of self-compassion. End the day's prayer with a conversation with Jesus. Pray to be grateful.

Five wounds

Oh my God
You have arms everywhere
thrown up
in squalid air

---

[1] Alberici, 'Whipping up fear to sway Brexit vote', *The Drum,* 21 June 2016.

Season One: Love

> as we violate each other.
> Five bullets
> nail him to ground
> just to 'show the bastards'.
> The fifth wound
> to make sure he is dead
> as dead can be.
>
> Five bullets wound
> the world,
> and innocence
> bleeds again.
>
> Look at the broken body.
> Feel the trembling fist on the trigger.
>
> Each wound in him –
> a wound in us.
>
> Perpetrator and consoler,
> I am powerless.
>
> I want to live in relentless love.
>
> Hope, forgive us.
> Enable us to forgive ourselves.

5. How do you feel towards people who have deeply offended you? How do you understand Matthew 26:24 when Jesus speaks of Judas: *'Better for that man had he never been born'*? Journal thoughts and feelings which you generally keep secret. This is your prayer today. You might choose to write poetry. Let the words lead you. The goal is not to write a masterpiece, but to explore your own thoughts on this strong statement.

6. God is present to you. Remember ways in which you have loved and been loved. Visit your patterns of guilt, and traps of shame. *Nothing can separate us from the love of God which is in Christ Jesus* (Romans 8:38–39).

7. Ponder the image 'Real Me' by Sieger Köder. You will find it online or in the book referenced below.[2] In what situations might your life patterns

---

[2] Simmonds, *The Closeness of God: The Art and Inspiration of Sieger Köder*, p. 54.

be related to suffering? What **disgrace** in yourself is an invitation to grace? Bring an important aspect of your pondering into the light of God's love. Stay in that for as long as it is helpful. How is God writing your story this week?

Sin

Like water,
it seeks its own level
in cracks and fissures
and seas.
No-one knows how deep it is
until they sink to the bottom.
There

        goodness is
dragged down.

Week Two

Prayer for your spiritual desires

What do you desire? This week, you are asked to pray for the grace to hear God's personal invitation of love to you. You could ask for the grace of humility in the face of God's unconditional, abundant love. You might ask to notice your own compassionate love or to increase your self-compassion. You might ask to be united with God in God's desires for this world.

Music
- Tyler Bates, 'Santiago de Compostela' from the motion picture, *The Way*. 2011.

Prayer focus for the days of the week

1. Re-read your recent journal. Are you beginning to notice any life-depleting patterns of thought or behaviour? However you see yourself (for example, as a struggling, flawed person on a journey, or a good person geared towards success) gauge your desire for God and pray to experience God's desire for you. Be with ever-present God who looks at you with generous love. Look to God as the source of all you are.

   Becoming

   The slow plough has exposed
   and plumped the soil.
   The sun gentles the surface.
   It is time to imagine
   the greening, soft hopefulness
   pushing through.

   I am willing to wait
   to feel the first movement of earth,
   the subtle threading of roots
   changing the deep story.

2. Luke 15:11–32. The son comes home to the prodigal father.

Spent

The father's hands were open,
so the decision was easy.
The son tied the money to his belt
for the adventure he was dreaming.

Sweet and irresistible pleasure,
a costly thing,
 like wine from late harvest,
numbs the senses for a while
until the stupor disappears –
a shadow of self remains.

The son was amongst the pigs,
lying there, his belly grunting,
the frothing forage in his mouth,
when he came to himself.

On callused feet he set off
for the fields his father's
hands had ploughed.

He saw him,
bent over, just like himself.
He felt his own breath sharp and shallow.

Wet-eyed and of slow gait,
he watched his father straighten
in hopeful recognition.

The father began to run,
 much faster than both thought he could,

arms outstretched,
embracing the timeless moment
of self-forgetting.

Robes, ring, and feet anointed,
they rested.

The villagers gathered around
the roasting calf

while the brother watched,
feeling his burden,
hands clenched
against the father's gift.

But the father, being
the only father he could be,
spoke:
My two sons,
 always,
all I have is yours.

3. Savouring prayer of day two: The father came out to meet both sons. *All I have is yours.* Also, ponder John 21:17. *Simon, son of John, do you love me?*

4. Can you imagine standing beside all that God loves, vowing your love and care? *Kanyini* (Australian aboriginal word) means connectedness. In the film 'Kanyini'[1] an aboriginal Anangu elder, Bob Randall, speaks of four types of connection which white invaders stole from the first custodians of Australia: connection to the land, connection to community and family, connection to history, and connection to 'Dreamtime' – the aboriginal worldview and spirituality which is intimately connected to place and country. The poem 'Kanyini' is a confession of guilt and shaming to aboriginal Australians. You might write your own 'Kanyini' poem or story.

Kanyini

My shadow is dark across the land.
I look down,
thrust upon you
my hatred of things black,
things which obstruct
what I want.

---

1 Hogan, 'Kanyini', 2006.

My shadow puts me on stilettos
strutting the earth.
It makes me run,
makes me speak too fast, too much,
makes me think
I can beat its growing
presence into night.
It is never noon-day

but for 38,000 years
before Christ,
night was not night for you.
Night was as the light,

black and blended
with the land, you belong –
keepers in the noon day
as midnight.

You are
the ochre of the land,
white witchetty grub,
honey of the ants,
emu on two feet,
hop of kangaroo.

Long the night
engulfed by my shadow, you
cannot find your way,
struggle to retrieve the ark in yourselves
when once you carried it.

It carried you.
Kanyini.
Heads held high
at one with nakedness and plenty,
drunk from the nipples of Kanyini.
Oh, mother earth.

No eyes can see.
No ears can hear Kanyini.
The heart grieves Kanyini.
The longing is Kanyini,
the spring and seasons
from which you know north and south,
west and east.

You are the land, decimated.
You are the prophet, passionate
voice in your body,
the spirit of truth
we try to discipline,
to whiten.

I listen.

The black prophet speaks
consoling words:
Lie down with your dark and flattened selves.
Be light as noon day.

5. Savouring prayer. 'If God takes note of our sins, which of us could survive such scrutiny?'[2]
   - Was there a challenging moment in your prayer this week? Was there a consoling moment? Today, explore one of these moments from a new perspective. Would music or art help you to deepen your experience of that moment? Journal about your interior movements.
6. As difficult as it may be, today you are invited to consider your own dying and death in the light of God's love. Imagine today as your last day; the place, the people, your feelings and thoughts. What is your sense of God? How are you with others? How might you be remembered?
   > Luke 7:36–50. The woman anoints Jesus. Search web images for the gospel reference, find a painting or representation that touches you in some way, and meditate on that image of this gospel event.
7. How are you feeling at the end of this week of contemplating Love in the face of sporadic human love? Return to the experiential poem

---

2 Simmonds, *The Closeness of God: The Art and Inspiration of Sieger Köder*, p. 67.

'Prepositioning God' and allow yourself to enter into the place which reflects how you would like to be with God today.

You could finish your week's prayer by taking a few words from your journal and drawing a ***mandala*** which expresses those words. The mandala is a 'container' of who you are at the time you create it. Use the colours and shapes which feel free and comfortable for you.

Week Three

Discernment of your interior movements

> 'Sin is necessary, but all will be well, and all will be well,
> and every kind of thing will be well'.[1]

Are you noticing an increasing awareness of your interior movements during your daily life? Perhaps some movements are uncomfortable and discordant, while others are light and peaceful. Note the permanence or impermanence of your interior movements; that is, which feelings are lasting and which are fleeting. Share with your spiritual director which movements lead to freedom and which movements seem to lead to **entrapment**.

Prayer for your spiritual desires

Pray for the gift of knowledge and a felt sense of being loved as you are.

Music

- Ólafur Arnalds and Alice Sara Ott, 'Letters of a Traveller' on the album *The Chopin Project*. Mercury Classics. 2015.

Prayer focus for the days of the week

1. Romans 8:35–39. Read several times.

    Recall a person in your life who has loved you. Savour the experience of being loved. Imagine the capacity of God's mysterious love to look upon you with love. Stay with the experience of being loved for as long as you are able.

2. Savouring prayer of day one. The poem below might remind you of an experience of being gazed upon with love. Ask for the grace to know the gaze of Love.

---

[1] Julian of Norwich. *Revelations of Divine Love*. 'Sin is behovely, but all shall be well, and all shall be well, and all manner of thing shall be well'. Ch. 27.

Portrait of the artist
In gratitude to Australian artist Dudley Drew (1924–2015)

What he sees, he sees,
I say with the mood
of a shoeless child,
naive in summer grass.

And he, poised,
like a sure-songed magpie scaling
note to note, red to violet,
touches brush on palette,
bewitched by Beethoven,
soft resonance swirling the air.
He gazes.

'What happened to you?'
pools on the canvas
in shadows not fully drenched.

His eyes dance from canvas to mirror.
Brow, like a vineyard
channeled in season,
resilient, focused,
living landscape.

He is small beside his hand
brush-stroking curves,
exploring neck to waist.
Violin passionate, tender.

And I, seen
with prodigal kindness,
am invited to be known
by the seamless heart
of Rembrandt's welcoming father.

3. Psalm 131. Like a child on the lap of Mother God. What is the grace you desire?

4. Savour the prayer of the previous day or pray with 'The sacrament of all things'.

   The sacrament of all things

   Abruptly and tenderly
   as I ready myself today, I hear
   Think of everything you do as a sacrament.
   I do not know what version or vision of myself,
   what sacramental hologram, I might be asked to be.
   But the words are clear:

   A sacrament is something one does.

   And are we not doing humanity?
   We breathe in and out, move, love, wonder, ponder,
   and other visible and invisible things.

   Think of everything you do as a sacrament.

   As something made present by the spirit,
   or the spirit unveiled by something,
   like the arrival of words heard through the seventh sense,
   and the mystery of humans with animals,
   bees communicating in the hive,
   and people hushed in sacramental calm.

5. Pilate asks Jesus, *'What is truth?'* (John 18:36–39). Enter into imaginative contemplation. Allow yourself to be present in the scene, as if it is happening now. If you can, be a participant, rather than an onlooker. Give yourself the freedom to imagine what it is like for you to be in that place. You are in God's presence. Let your imagination lead you without censure. Engage the physical senses and the spiritual senses. (Check the Glossary for **application of the senses.**) In your journal today, write and reflect on your imaginative contemplation of this scene, noticing what happened, how you felt, what you thought, how others looked at you. Which inner movements draw you to life and love and which drive you away from life and love?

6. Savour the prayer of the previous day. If you want further material, read *Becoming Conscious* in the additional material at the end of this book.
7. Savouring day. Reread your week's journal, recalling the graced and disgraced patterns of your life. Bring the graces to bear on the disgraces, allowing God's light to transform you. You do not have to work hard. Your desire and God's love are enough.

Gaze

Eyes on God.
Two pointers to the moon.

Season Two: Intimacy

Come in

I invite God inside
And find God is already there

Introduction

Season Two: Intimacy invites you to an ever-deepening consciousness of God within. The focus of the retreat turns to the narrative of Jesus' life, beginning with God's dream for him, Mary's conception, his birth, his early and his public life, leading to his last visit to Jerusalem in which he shared supper with friends. As Season Two unfolds, it is punctuated by joy and sadness, healings and disappointments.

Season Two is the longest of the four seasons. There will be repetition of some of the prayer material including quotes from the Ignatian Spanish Autograph text of the *Spiritual Exercises*, translated by Elder Mullan SJ. The repetitions are an opportunity to deepen the prayer experience. Ignatius frequently encourages repetitions in prayer. What he means by the word 'repetition' is actually 'deepening' or 'savouring'.

In following the pathway of your life through Season Two, notice how you feel about walking with Jesus through cycles of friendship, compassion, celebration and loss. What is it like for you to have the companionship of Jesus, who knows completely what it is to be human in a troubled political and religious climate? What do you think it is like for Jesus to have your companionship?

Poetry

Again, the poetry will invite you to connect with your own life story; some poems reflect more closely upon the life of Jesus as narrated in the gospels, and other poems are about everyday life. The poems are actually invitations to connection. Perhaps you might feel moved to write your own poems.

Music
- Kimberly and Alberto Rivera, 'Hear the Sound' on the album *Pneuma*. RiveraSong Publishing. 2014.

Consolation and Desolation

Spiritual consolation and **spiritual desolation** have their specific character for each person. The exercises will help you notice which patterns in your life are helpful and which are unhelpful; which patterns contribute energy and love to your world, and which patterns are obstacles to energy and love.

smog choke
fractures light
sunset

The modified haiku poem, 'smog choke ...' suggests that even our flaws in some way contribute to the beautiful persons we will become.

Just as unhelpful patterns of thinking and feeling have taken years to develop, they can sometimes take a long time to dismantle. Ignatius encourages patience. It is helpful to take the long view and accept yourself in the process.

Discernment

The poem 'Light dirt' is clear about the characteristics of strong, life-giving discernment.

Light dirt

You are in the right dirt if it is light dirt;
if you feel earthed, grounded, and you are steady;
if the dirt is sacred and you are thankful
that you have the privilege of being there;
walking that way, treading that path, at your pace,
using your skill, your talents;
and your life feels bigger and richer,
spacious and free. You are consoled
with God as your companion, sustainer, enabler,
and you can look in the eyes of the people you meet
to find Christ there, blessing you
with more blessing than you are giving.
You are in the right dirt if it is light dirt
and you are happy to take off your shoes,
and feel the touch of your earth-work
with nothing between you and God's desire;
finding something joyous about the mud or the sand,
something life giving, energising.

You know you are in your right dirt when you are free
to say you are tired, that you need a break,
and that although you are skilled and good at your work,
too much of it turns you from God instead of to God;
You are in the right dirt when you discover the place within
where you are already kind, compassionate, and balanced.
You know you are in the right dirt when your heart beats
in union with God, in communion with all.

Writing your own poem

Many people feel intimidated by poetry and especially by the suggestion that they write their own, so I will take you, step by step, through creating a 'word image' of yourself. Take an A4 sheet of paper and fill the page with a drawing like the one below.

- From reading your own journal, select a phrase which moves you in some way.
- Write these words in the middle of the flower.
- Ponder the words in your heart until another word or phrase comes to

you.

- Write these new word(s) in one of the petals.
- Return to your initial phrase in the centre of the flower, and wait until another word or phrase emerges. Write it in another petal.

There is no need to edit your words – leave them as raw entries, even if you do not understand them yourself. Repeat this exercise until you are satisfied with what you have written. Together, the phrases in the flower form the basis of your poem.

- Now write these phrases and words in any order, under each other as you would in writing a list.
- Add or subtract words as you please.
- Read your whole poem and give it a title.

You now have a word-image or poem about yourself at this point in time. Reflect on it. Write in your journal how you feel in relation to the poem. Allow God to speak to you through the poem.

This is an exercise you can do at any time.

Imaginative gospel contemplation

Season Two: Intimacy invites you to contemplation as a significant pathway to encountering Jesus Christ and the Mystery of God. Imaginative gospel contemplation is a tool of self-revelation and self-understanding. As you allow your imagination to lead, you enter the scene of the text, positioning yourself within it, and running your senses over it: What is the place and environment like in your imagination? How is the weather today? Do you notice colours and sounds? What about the smells and taste in the air? What are you doing? Who is there? Are there conversations taking place? What is being said? Are you involved in those conversations? Have you noticed, for example, what Jesus is like, how he approaches and speaks to people, and how he speaks to you? How are you in relation to him?

As you write your reflections in your journal, you are developing your contemporary gospel.

Visiting your spiritual director

In your ongoing visits with your spiritual director, you will find that, primarily, she listens as you share your experiences of prayer. You can share anything that puzzles, troubles or affirms you. Your spiritual director will not judge you as you attend to 'graced' or 'disgraced' experiences. He will help you to savour your heartfelt interior movements of consolation. She will wonder with you as you explore movements of spiritual desolation.

Beginning your prayer of Season Two

As previously, begin your prayer hour each day by taking the time you need to refocus your attention on the prayer you are about to begin. A simple exercise in which you name what you are about to do can be sufficient. This exercise is similar to Grace, a prayer we might pray before we eat.

Become aware of how you feel in coming to prayer. Use a centering tool such as the prayer poem 'Prepositioning God' or a physical exercise which gathers and focuses energy, or a mantra such as, 'I am who I am. You are who you are.' The act of sitting in a supportive chair, feet flat on the floor, hand with palms up, one on top of the other, and paying attention to your breathing is prayer itself. Noticing the warmth or coolness of breath moving in and out your nostrils helps to connect you to your source of life. The simple sound of a gong filling your surrounds can bring peace and quiet joy, enjoining you to all things.

It is helpful to take time over the meditations. If at first you are slow to enter the prayer, know that 'showing up' to prayer is more important than how effective it feels.

Savouring prayer

Savouring prayer returns you to difficult, challenging or consoling elements of a previous prayer that offered some spiritual insight or invitation. Ignatius tells us that 'it is not in knowing much, but realising and relishing things interiorly that contents and satisfies the soul'. [2]

Drawing a mandala is a useful tool of self-expression and self-knowledge. The mandala circle is the 'container' which holds who you are in God. The contents might appear abstract or literal. You might use a mandala as a way of deepening your experience of savouring your prayer.

Week One

Prayer for your spiritual desires

The grace you seek in Season Two is to know Jesus intimately, love Jesus more truly and intensely, and follow Jesus so that you and Jesus share congruent desires and goals. This framework helps the prayer but the specific outcomes of your prayer vary from day to day, and from person to person.

In week one of Season Two, Ignatius wants us to transition from Season One with a meditation inviting us to ponder the kind of leadership to which we are drawn. In the Ignatian *Spiritual Exercises*, this meditation is named 'The Call of the King' [91]. The text below, 'Pondering possibilities and two leadership styles' offers a scenario which includes elements of the 'Call of the King' [91] and the 'Meditation on Two Standards' [136–146] from the *Spiritual Exercises*.

Communion of the faithful

A further suggestion is that you ponder who, among your loved ones, you would like to recruit on this journey with you through the life, death and resurrection cycles of the spiritual exercises. This notion is drawn from the Communion of the Faithful, which is underpinned by the belief that life is eternal, and so we can always request living or dead spiritual companions for our life journeys. Ignatius was in the practice of asking Mary, the Mother of Jesus, to take up this role with him [63].

Journal

Record some important movements experienced in prayer. This is more than a record of your prayer; it is prayer itself. Through your journal, you might continue your conversation with God or you might gain some insight from your writing. Journal writing is an important part of praying the spiritual exercises.

Music
- Audrey Assad, 'I shall not want' on the album *A Fortunate Fall*. 2013.

Sustenance prayer

Reveal to me your power, God.
>Inspire me
>by the universe, moon, planets and stars.

Reveal your presence.
>Activate my memory of all that is good.
>Help me to see where hope grows.
>Show me seeds of kindness,
>exchanges of joy,
>moments of courage.

Reveal your vulnerability.
>Let me see you Jesus,
>Christ incarnated,
>in my neighbour,
>in myself.
>Nurture love and compassion in me.

Give me this day my daily bread
>so the best of me can grow.

Amen.

Prayer focus for the days of the week

1. Pondering possibilities and two leadership styles

   Consider the first scenario:

   Imagine a scenario, a place, an historic period in which a good leader is trying to exercise leadership with kindness, offering full participation to others to achieve set goals and outcomes. The pivotal goal is dominance in a competitive environment. This leader invites you to relinquish everything for the cause. You have two choices available – you can say *yes* or *no*.

   If you say *yes*, you will share the benefits of success just as you have shared in the labour towards that success. If you say *no*, however, you will be unwelcome and ostracised. Imagine standing before this leader being offered this opportunity. Who is there as you stand before the leader who seeks your response? What is the conversation like? How are you responding? Will you say *yes* or *no*?

Consider the second scenario:

The second scenario is similar to the first, except that the leader is Christ Jesus, having gospel values and expecting holy outcomes. The goal is to work towards overcoming inequalities at every level of life. If you say *yes* to participate in his labour, love will become the milieu in which all thoughts, words and actions occur from now on. If you say 'no', you will walk away knowing that the invitation is always open to you.

Imagine Jesus as a loving leader. What might love look like? Could it look like an aboriginal elder practising a spirituality in which all belong to each other, to shared history, ancestors and progeny, as well as the land on which all live? This practice would be in opposition to a democracy in which status, wealth and possessions are distributed and owned according to, for example, country of birth, education and influence. What else might love look like?

Do you recognise these opposing models operating in your life or in our world? What might a world underpinned by love look like? What are your desires to contribute to a world underpinned by love? Who would be your leader? If you say *yes*, what would you offer such a leader? What will you offer Christ Jesus?

Prayer: Glory be to Creative God, to Jesus Christ, Leader and Lover, and to the Spirit of God companioning us in all of life. Amen.

2. Savour the prayer of day one. 'The call' offers a succinct way of savouring yesterday's prayer.

The call

It is quite simple really. We are called to love –
to compassion for the dismissed self,
to help others to love themselves,
to companion the unfolding of love –
the union of self-giving and self-fulfilling love.

How one does this, matters little
for love is above all things, in all things.

> Love purifies and embraces all things
> until all things are indistinguishable
> from the love which permeates them.

- Is God speaking to you?
- Speak with God about today's prayer.

Prayer: Glory be to Creative God, to Jesus Christ, Leader and Lover, and to the Spirit of God companioning us in all of life. Amen.

3. Luke 1:26–38. The Incarnation and the Annunciation. Imagine how God's loving presence in the cosmos impacts all things and brings about the totality of creative life that Love is intended to bring. Ponder the divine Mystery's creative imagination in Jesus Christ's entry and presence on earth in Israel. You might begin to read *God-with-her,* a poem from day four this week.

> Read the Biblical text twice. The first time is a simple reading for meaning, and the second time, try to become a part of the narrative. Then put your text down and let your imagination take you to the province of Galilee and the details of the place where Mary received the angelic vision. Notice the place, people and conversation.
>
> When you are satisfied that your imaginative contemplation is complete, consider how it was for you. How did you feel towards the characters? What thoughts did you have? Was there anything new that emerged from this narrative for you? Was there any familiar pattern of response that is jarring or consoling for you? What might you want to share with God? Can you listen to what God might desire for you? Do you want to have a conversation with Mary or Gabriel? How do you want to respond?

Music

- Ignatius suggests that you finish the contemplation with the Lord's prayer. You could pray with Lisa Gerrard and Patrick Cassidy, 'Abwoon' (The 'Our Father' in Aramaic) on the album *Immortal Memory*, 2004. Or you could pray the sustenance prayer presented earlier in this week's activities.
4. Using the poem 'God-with-her', savour your prayer on the Annunciation.[1]

---

[1] See also the poem 'Consent' by Denise Levertov, in *Breathing the Water.*

God-with-her

Mary draws back when Gabriel appears.
Confused, Mary forgets
she longs for love, for God
who offers more than she has ever known.

But Mary returns to herself.
Her heart leaps in God's embrace.
She no longer feels the boundaries of herself.
She is stilled in the eternal moment.
There are no words
to speak the way beyond
all other ways of being one.

Gabriel, blessed confidant of God's desires,
you recede as Mary says *yes*.

Bearer of the promise,
what happens in your heart

as you witness her grappling heart?

Finish the prayer in the usual way, noting always what has disturbed you on the one hand or brought life to you, on the other. Would you like to offer a prayer of gratitude?

5. Luke 1:39–56. The visit of Mary to Elizabeth.

Suddenly aware

Mary visited Elizabeth.
The child in Elizabeth's womb
leapt for joy.

Suddenly conscious
of faith and heritage
brought down through centuries.

Discernment is an easy thing
when love leaps.

6. Matthew 1:18–25. Joseph's dream.
7. Savouring day. Ponder moments in your week's prayer.

Week Two

Prayer for your spiritual desires

As you know from last week's prayer, the grace for which you are praying in this season is to know, love and follow Christ. There may be other graces you desire. Name them also. Notice how you feel about intentionally praying for a particular grace.

This week, you are offered the short poem 'Kardia'. Although **kardia** ($καρδία$ Gk feminine noun) is literally translated from the Greek word as 'heart', in the scriptures *kardia* does not refer to the heart as the organ which animates the blood supply to the body. Rather it speaks poetically of the centre and seat of life in a person. It is used in this week as a way of understanding the application of the senses.

Journal

For the entire retreat, continue with your journal record of the movements experienced during prayer.

Application of the senses

Ignatius encouraged retreatants to use their bodily senses as a way of entering into their spiritual senses. This is the process implied in *'Taste and see that the Lord is sweet'* (Psalm 33:9).

> **Kardia**
>
> I come to You
> by way of the senses,
> to perceive with interior vision,
> hear with ear of the heart,
> comprehend things inexpressible.
>
> I am simply held.

Imaginative contemplation

In imaginative contemplation, read the text twice. The first reading is intended for you to become familiar with the narrative. The second reading is to help you become immersed in the narrative. After the second reading, it might be helpful to close your Bible and simply allow the narrative, as you recall it, to come to life for you. Stay with your prayer for as long as it holds your attention.

At the end of your prayer: a reminder

- Listen to what God might be saying to you.
- Have a conversation with God about today's prayer.
- Write in your journal which interior movements were significant for you.
- Pray a prayer of gratitude.

Music

- Jorge Mendéz, 'Life Within' on the album *Silhouettes*. 7 DigitalCanada. 2013.

Body

Try a simple Tai Chi or Qigong exercise. You will easily find an example on the internet. Choose one which gathers your scattered energy into your soul-space.

Prayer focus for the days of the week

1. Matthew 4:18–25. Call of the disciples.
2. Philippians 2:5–11. Humility is the grace to want to follow Christ in your heart. Pray again with the poem, 'The sacrament of all things' from Season One, week three.
3. Luke 2:1–7. Travel to Bethlehem. Preparing to give birth.
4. Ignatius encourages imaginative contemplation and the application of the senses within your prayer on the birth of Jesus.
5. Luke 2:8–20. The birth of Jesus. A favourite Christmas carol might also be meaningful to you.

Season Two: Intimacy

Aural banquet

Magpie and thrush stir
feathers on a stave.
Shepherd wakes from dream,
touches fragrant heaven's throng,
lingers in her light.
O sound-filled night.

Holy
bleat of settling sheep,
squeak of dewy grass,
whispering purple curse
and the gamboling lamb who follows
the shepherd's seamless moves
in clear starry light.
Thin beam of stable flame.
Graced night.

Shepherd tiptoes to the door ajar,
hears a lively cry,
the shiver of a mother
and a father's lullaby.

Night of hope
flocks with joy.
Shepherd's heart holds
a stable for the shepherd-king.

6. Matthew 2:1–12. Herod sends the Magi in search of the Promised One.

Magi

Arabian visionaries
chart the stars,
look beyond
the vast vault above,
sense the mystery
they cannot chart,
and follow.

7. Savour any part of your week's prayer.

   Baby's first breath

   In her first breath,
   through wide and eager mouth,
   baby draws whatever comes;
   whatever fills the emptiness
   of that first hunger.
   In the cells of her tiny self, baby
   distinguishes oxygen, the lesser
   part of air, to cool the crying need,
   And the universal spirit comes in
   to dance greater and lesser steps,
   filling her with baby-ness, and all
   she needs to be herself.
   And, at the going out,
   her mother's breath resumes
   warm streams of consolation,
   babbling aspiration,
   inspiration,
   and the universe is changed.

8. Savouring prayer of the week. 'Goddess poem' is an application of the senses poem.

Season Two: Intimacy

Goddess poem[1]

Go inside the poem.
Feel the warmth, the
roomy safety. Feel her
boundaries yield, stretch,
to accommodate your flips
and turns your struggle to
find the comfy space, the
just right holding. Listen to
sounds familiar and muffled
and rounded lullaby rhythms
growing inside you, nurturing
your voice, your claim to be
heard, to be silent. Go inside
the poem. Feel your body
move with fear and love.
Retrieve the slippery
traces in the poem
you know the
poem we all
know

---

1 Marburg. 'Goddess poem' previously known as 'Goddess prayer' *Grace Undone. Love*, p. 29.

Week Three

Ignatius tells us that 'It is not in knowing much but realising and relishing things interiorly that contents and satisfies the soul' [2]. Are you beginning to discover this reality in your prayer experience? Continue to speak with God about your prayer each day, listening as Elijah did, to the 'delicate, whispering voice' of God (1 Kings 19:11–13)

Praying for the grace

The three sage-astronomers who followed the star to find Jesus are traditionally known as the 'magi'. The **magis** (Latin) literally means 'the more' and, in the context of Ignatian spirituality, *magis* is understood as 'more for Christ'. If you are drawn to the *magis*, you are always seeking more freedom, more grace, more holy desire, more love, and you are also seeking to embody your graced desire. The sage-astronomers are models for us as they travel towards 'the more'. This week, pray with them to be 'the more' through knowing, loving and following Christ.

> **To the margins**
>
> Magi are wise
> enough to know
> their certain ignorance.
>
> Drawn to the *magis*,
> they long, rather than know.
>
> They follow a star,
> stirring light
> in their hearts
> more than the sky,
>
> To the margins, where
> sheep and goats lose their footing,
> they make a silent journey,
> growing in hope

that the child within
and the Child without
will recognise each other.

Music
- Sissel, 'Carrier of the Secret' on the album *All Good Things*. Mercury. 2002.

Body
Apps such as 'Smiling Mind' offer suggestions for stilling the mind through engaging the body.

Prayer focus for the days of the week
1. Luke 2:22–38. Jesus' parents go to the Temple in Jerusalem to present Jesus to Yahweh, their God, in the presence of the just and devout man, Simeon. The prophet, Anna praises God for the child, Jesus.
2. Savour the prayer of day one.
3. Matthew 2:13–18. Joseph's dream warns of Herod's proposed search and murder of Jesus.
4. Savour the prayer of day three.

Indigenous?

I have known no land but this;
loved none other.
Am I indigenous too? Primitive roots
in red earth, muddy river
length, height, breadth and depth
of my white body. I know
the umbilical longing
for milk and honey;
thirst for my land.
I hear the voice of my ancestors
asking for faithfulness.
I do not long to belong,
I belong.

5. Matthew 2:19–23. Joseph, Mary and Jesus return from Egypt to Nazareth.
6. Savour the prayer of day five.

   At nine

   When I was small,
   wonder-joy was given.
   I lay warm in my bed,
   feeling my heart beat,
   looking at myself from the ceiling,
   expanding the world I knew,
   musing the mystery of becoming
   one
   amidst millions of permutations.
   I am no-one else.

7. Savour the prayers of the week. Re-engage with experience(s) from your week of prayer.

Week Four

Preparation for prayer

Centering yourself for prayer can happen in many ways. This is a simple way: interlock the fingers of each hand, and circle your thumbs around each other until you feel calm, and then let go of the movement.

Prayer for your spiritual desires

In this week's prayer you are asked to consider choices and values. Ignatius puts before us a meditation which asks us to consider two contrasting value systems. This week, as you follow the early life of Jesus, you might wonder about how Jesus' values developed, and you might pray to embrace the values of Jesus in your own authentic calling. To pray for the grace to know, love and follow Christ is to choose your own authentic life.

Music

- Steffany Gretzinger, 'Letting Go' on the album *The Undoing*. Bethel Music. 2014.

Prayer focus for the days of the week.

1. Luke 2:39–40; 51–52. Use imaginative contemplation as you pray with the texts from Jesus' childhood years.
2. Savour the prayer of day one.
3. Luke 2:41–50. Engage in imaginative contemplation of Jesus and his parents as they travel to Jerusalem for the feast of Passover.
4. Savour the prayer of day three.

> **In the Father's house**
>
> Did you not know?
> Did you not know I must be?
> Did you not know I must be in my Father?
> Did you not know I must be in my Father's house?
> Did you not know I must be in the Father and the Father in me?

5. Check the Glossary as needed for a brief explanation of 'spiritual consolation' and 'spiritual desolation'.

   Pray, using the following poem as an adaptation of the meditation on Ignatius' Two Standards and Two Value Systems, presented in Season Two, week one. Alternatively, remember a situation of your own in which you experienced interior moral conflict. You might choose a personal experience or a response to a world event. You are being asked in the meditation to decide between two choices, two values. How do you imagine God is looking at you while you consider these choices?

   Friday 8 pm in Chinatown

   Through the picture window
   in Latrobe Lane, we see her
   post-pubescent poverty,
   blue-white skin pressed against her bones,
   lifting her knitted mini-dress above her waist,
   her knickers to her ankles.
   She squats beside the rubbish bin,
   relieves herself;
   the cloned friend helpless
   to create a cubicle.
   My husband locks eyes with me,
   closets us against a crass response.
   We eat our banquet, wondering
   when she had her last meal, and
   if she has had it.

6. Savour the poem, 'Raising the standard' on Two Standards and Two Values.

   Raising the standard

   My 'yes' to God's standard
   does not have a standardised outcome.
   My 'yes' does not put me in a peripheral place
   But draws me to the centre of myself.
   1. Savouring day using the application of the senses.

Week Five

Introduction

How are you living with the Principle and Foundation at this stage of the spiritual exercises? The Principle and Foundation expresses some beliefs about how to live at balance with all things; wanting neither one thing nor another, unless it is in collaboration with God. This is the way that Jesus approached his public life, from his baptism to his apprehension in the Garden of Gethsemane and finally to his death.

Preparation for prayer

As a way of drawing into prayer this week, take a pencil and draw a wide circle on a sheet of paper, keeping your pencil on the page at all times. Spiral inwards at a comfortable pace, until you reach the centre.

Prayer for your spiritual desires

From this point onward in the retreat, watch Jesus to see how he responds to the situations and people who come your way in your imagination or your reality. How does he respond to you?

This week, the grace for which to pray is to know, love and follow Christ as Jesus begins this public journey. This grace is also to know the difference between God's way and the way of the ego.

Music

- The Ten Tenors, 'Water' (Va Pensiero) on the album *Tenology. The Best So Far* Limited Christmas edition, by The Ten Tenors and Benny Ulvaeus, Bjorn Anderson, Stig Andersson. 2006.

Meditation: Two Values

It is not uncommon to find that the disordered part of you is your strength gone awry. In fact it is more than possible that your worst 'disgrace' is the invitation to an extraordinary grace. The poem 'Two Sides' lists possible life-depleting patterns and their opposites. You could write your personal 'Two Sides' prayer to form part of your daily exercise as you pray for the grace to follow Christ. 'Two sides' is an interpretation of the ***Ignatian meditation***, Two Standards and Two Values.

Two sides

Loving God,
may we seek to be inspirational
when we are in the limelight.

May we lead as disciples,
ambitious for you.

May we accumulate ways of service
if we are wealthy,

and may we be rich in love
if we are poor.

May we hold fast to our authenticity
if we are stubborn.

May we value others' words
if we are talkers.

If we are withdrawn,
help us to recede into You.

If we are judgmental,
may we become discerning.

If we are humble,
make us proud of You.

If we are suspicious,
may we be vigilant for You.

If we are planners,
may we trust the journey.

If we are practical,
help us to be creative.

If we have all the answers,
may we become wise.

In all our charred endeavours,
may we find a fire burning.

Amen.

Prayer focus for the days of the week

1. Matthew 3:13–17. The baptism of Jesus in the Jordan River.

   With what can I baptise you, Jesus?

   My heart is water thinking of it.
   All is pure compared to me, yet
   You come.

   You desire
   to receive
   my word
   shaky, unrefined,
   crying in my wilderness

   to receive
   my blessing.
   Wounded, weeping
   longing for You,
   Your touch,

   here I am
   to affirm You
   Your mighty call.

   My baptism is a whisper.

2. Savour the prayer of day one.
3. Matthew 4:1–11. Engage in imaginative contemplation of Jesus' temptation in the desert.
4. Savour the prayer of day three.

Vessels are hollow

Wedged and thrown, the ball of clay
spins, plays in liquid hands.
Mastery of thumbs and fingers
persuade perfect balance, symmetry,
a rearrangement of raw earth
rising against natural forces
forming a hollow the clay anticipates, desires.
Its character awaits this test, this moment,
every moment.

The potter senses through clay-skin and
cracked and muscled hands, through
terracotta under fingernails,
a thrilling urgent shaping,
an accelerating wheel, a dizzy race.

But she dreams of
molten clay,
explosions in the kiln,
sentinels on pedestals,
warnings,
and finally
a settled fearless voice
heard beneath it all.

Daybreak verge,
she bypasses the wheel,
stands before studio shelves,
selects the crazed, wide-mouthed raku pot;
an ornament, hand-built, once-fired.
She smiles
at each face in turn,
listens to each line and incline speak.
She prepares a generous glaze,
patient green in its hollow.

Season Two: Intimacy

A second firing, risking, cooling.

She runs her finger-tips
over the rough and tepid surface,
raises the pot to the light,
examines its interior for cracks, flaws.
She smells the pot,
takes breath from its hollow.

She speaks into it
and from it;
an ornament no more,
a ready vessel.

1. Contemplate Two Values. You might choose to use the following poem as a way of thinking about values, rules and policies.

   Thirst

   In the clinic, the derelict
   was fraught with fever, enough
   to make a dog salivate. I
   X-rayed him, asked him to wait.

   He panted, disturbed his
   burdened chest, coughed
   from somewhere deep,
   and asked for water.

   With the narrow door open, he sat
   on the bench in the cubicle.
   He was small in the room
   of toilet dimensions.
   Dehydrated flesh sagged from his bones.

   He fiddled with clothes, confused
   about the order of things.
   His watch had stopped.

   My eyes are gritty, he said,
   as if it was a question.

Then he dressed himself, dizzy
with checks and holes.

I washed my hands.

He waited on the verandah
for the rain or something to pass –

> I did.

Could you take me to the station?

Sorry. It's against policy.

He understood 'policy'
referenced daily
to his exact, polite pleading.

Sorry pulled at my mind
until re-shaped,
I stopped the car,
motioned him to approach.

His eyes
in habitual reverence,
honoured me in a way that
shamed my fear.

He sat in the front.
I drove to the station
talking a rehearsed narrative.

But when he said *bless you*,

I received the cup of water,
astonished by my thirst.

5. Luke 4:14–22. Engage in imaginative contemplation on the spirit of God within Jesus Christ.
6. Savour the week's prayers.

Week Six

Prayer for your spiritual desires

This week focuses on choices and decisions. Sometimes desires elude us and we might need to pray simply for the desire to desire what is best for us. Ask God to show you what it means to know, love and follow Christ. You will know what that grace is as you accompany Jesus. For what grace specifically would you like to pray this week?

Music
- Bebo Norman, 'Wine from Water' on the album *Lights of Distant Cities*. 2012.

Prayer focus for the days of the week
1. Making decisions from available choices. Choices are available options from which a person might decide. What are the options presented to you so far during the prayers of the spiritual exercises? Which decisions have lead to love, joy, peace, patience, kindness, goodness, faithfulness, gentleness and self-control (Galatians 5:22–23)? Read the poem, 'Dreaming a grace' in the additional material.
2. Savour the prayer of day one.
3. Mark 1:16–20. Seeing and calling fishermen.
4. Savouring prayer or 'phases and phrases'.

   phases and phrases

   the sentence without punctuation is so tense with phrases and savouring prayers and the same conjunction frequently attaching disparate clauses of his life story that he cannot remember that he is the subject there is not even a comma to pause in the drama to help him find out what is happening to him and when he is finally stopped his life blood the ink almost dried he voices a question that inverts subject and predicate why did the world not speak to me of mountains and bees of fountains and apostrophes of babies and smiles of maybes and whiles and when he pauses from asking the predicate reciprocates and stops him fully in wonder finding the subject a thing of beauty too

5. Read 'Three couples'. In considering the couples' different attitudes to life, observe your responses, noticing where you are drawn; where the *kardia*-life within you is most consoled and integrated. Dialogue with your own wisdom. Take time to have a conversation with God, with Jesus, or another person you have loved.

Three couples

Three married sisters with their partners routinely buy a Tattslotto syndicate ticket each week. One week, the ticket won a substantial amount of money, so the couples shared the prize equally.

The win caused each couple to think about the morality of receiving and having so much money. They were not sure what to do. So they came together a few weeks later to discuss their fortune and their ideas about what might be the best way to manage this potentially life-changing amount of money.

Couple One

This couple want to rid themselves of the money by giving it to a worthy charity, but while their intentions are good, they defer the decision to relinquish the money, meanwhile enjoying their ongoing wealth and the status that comes with it.

Couple Two

This couple want theoretically to do what is best with the windfall, but they also have an attachment to the lifestyle it offers, so much so that they do not seek to know what options are possible and do not really want to know the action to which God might be inviting them.

Couple Three

This third couple want to rid themselves of the money. They do not yet know what to do with the money so they wait on God to show them. They do not want the money to interfere with their deeper priority to live in relationship with God.

6. John 2:1–11. Read the passage twice. Pray your own imaginative contemplation. 'The Marriage feast' in the additional material is an imaginative contemplation which departs significantly from the scriptural text.
7. Savouring day or Examen of the week. Are you finding it helpful to gather the graces through the Examen prayer? Pray for guidance and give thanks to God for who you are and who God is to you.

Week Seven

Prayer for your spiritual desires

This week the grace sought is to have the courage to respond wholeheartedly to the invitation to know, love and follow Christ.

Music
- Margaret Maria and Gabriel Pulido-Cejudo, 'Prayer of Hope' on the album *Believe*. (Sound induced signature motifs.) [A Woman's Health Initiative] iBioSign Health Integrated Systems Corporation. 2015.

Prayer focus for the days of the week
1. John 21:15–18. Jesus asks, *Do you love me?*
2. Savour the prayer of day one.
3. Mark 10:17–31. Jesus looks at the rich young man with love.

> **Variants of brown**
>
> I woke late; the heat already burning the grass.
>
> I was served gefilte fish, wood-fired bread,
> honey, figs and raw almonds.
> Smiling
>
> I remembered my friend Daniel's musings,
>
> *Is Jesus of Nazareth a sage or prophet?*
> *Could he be the Promised One?*
> *He has new ideas about eternal life.*
> *Mere men cannot teach such things.*
>
> Dressed in embroidered linen and leather sandals,
> I asked the servants to equip the horses.
> I wanted to see at first hand
> what the frenzy was about.

Season Two: Intimacy

A homogenous voice
and variants of brown greeted us.
And then I saw him. Jesus.

The itinerant drew pity and curiosity from me.
I was touched by his simplicity,
and quickly dismounted on the pathway made for me.

Strangely, I felt impelled to kneel.
Words tumbled out, *Good Teacher,
what must I do to inherit eternal life?*

He gave a Rabbi's answer,
quoting commandments given to Moses,
our great ancestor from a thousand years ago.

Jesus said, *But, why do you call me good?
No-one is good but God alone.*

I replied, *My servants call me Good Master.
I follow the commandments.*

No-one is good but God alone, Jesus repeated.

His gaze, a river from his soul

flowed into me.
I felt at once
I had never been truly loved.

*You lack one thing; go, sell what you own,
and give the money to the poor,
and you will have treasure in heaven;
Then come, follow me,* he said.

In that moment, my shoulders bore
all the world's possessions,
the pain of losing my wife's respect,
and the honour I hold in this region.

The crowd waited.

But I was voiceless, naked.

4. Mark 12:41–44. The widow's offering
5. Matthew 4:23—5:12. Jesus Christ's value system.
6. Savour the prayer of day five.
7. Savouring day. Reflect on the week's graces and obstacles to grace.

Week Eight

This week, you go on a pilgrimage with Jesus throughout the region of Judea and beyond the Jordan River where you will meet Bartimaeus, Zacchaeus and the disturbed man from Gerasa. You will also accompany Jesus as he is tested by Jewish officials on his knowledge of the Torah. Notice how you respond to each of the characters in your imaginative contemplations on the texts.

Prayer for your spiritual desires
The grace for which you are asked to pray is to know, love and follow Jesus. How are you feeling as you accompany Jesus into challenging situations?

Music
- Alisa Hopper, 'All I see is you' on the album *Encounter*. All Music. 2007.

Prayer focus for the days of the week
1. Mark 10:46–52. A blind person hears, *'What do you want?'* What do you hear?

   Bartimaea

   What do you want me to do for you?
   For you, Bartimaea?

   Blindness creeps in
   a lengthy twilight falling
               into
                         darkness.
   It is too late to practise counting the steps
   from home to the gates of Jericho
   where people with infirmity beg.

   I am Bartimaea, cloaked in culture.
   My skirts are sprinkled
   with piteous, pious offerings.

I feel tremors through the earth;
people moving around me
in unwitting disregard.

I sense disgust, fear and anger.
I am comforted, fingering the gravel on the roadway.
I smell the dust on my clothes,
fibres textured with wear,
familiar tassels on my cloak,
the knots I stroke.
Crinkly strands separate and straighten.

Hope is submerged most of the time.
I am grateful for harsh words.
They give me a sense of direction.

The occasional tone of compassion
and the curiosity of children
affirm I exist.
 Yes, I exist –
I am hungry and thirsty.

I tune into stories about the Nazarene.
I hear he is on his way. Jesus is his name.
And when he passes,
I stun myself, calling for mercy,
so loudly that I cannot decipher
the mocking words all around me.

Jesus is close to me.
He speaks into my ear.
What do you want me to do for you?
For you, Bartimaea?

How does he know my name?
Isn't it obvious what I want?
But the question makes me wonder,
what do I want?

The sun is strong and warm,
and a breeze is playful on my face.
The question is as harp and flute together.

Season Two: Intimacy

>His voice comes to bear on how I see things.
>
>My voice rises from the blind crowd.

2. Savour the prayer of day one. What do you want?
3. Luke 8:26–39. Jesus and the disturbed man from Gerasa.
4. Savour the prayer of day three.

   On the margins

   >Jesus Christ in the margins
   >makes the margins central.

5. Luke 19:1–10. Zacchaeus climbs a tree to see Jesus.
6. Savour the prayer of day five.

   The moment

   >He climbs the sycamore tree,
   >secretes himself amongst the foliage.
   >His eyes, shining like blackened leaves,
   >look over one solid mass of people.
   >He sees long dark hair and veils,
   >clothes and colours,
   >shawls backing away.
   >He watches the children move
   >nimbly through tunics and skirts.
   >He hears the rising sound.
   >Dissenters and believers turn
   >towards the tree. Tall
   >men stand taller
   >as he shrinks behind a branch.
   >
   >The years have slowed this moment.
   >He shuffles along the branch
   >and at the end he sees
   >one face looking up
   >
   >at him.

7. Savouring day.

Week Nine

This week you are presented with three kinds of humility. Do you have a definition of humility? To what kind of humility could you aspire?

Prayer for your spiritual desires

This week, pray for a deepening awareness and practice of humility in your life. The grace is to trust Jesus to accompany you and guide you. It is the grace to trust Christ within.

Music
- Christopher Young, 'Humility and Love' on the motion picture album *Creation*. Lakeshore Records. 2016.

Prayer focus for the days of the week

1. Read and ponder 'Three kinds of humility'.

   ### Three kinds of humility

   ### The first kind

   I seek to obey the law of God, the ten commandments. I aspire to avoid the 'seven deadly sins (vices)' which are: greed, gluttony, lust, envy, sloth, wrath, pride. I seek to be balanced and moderate, generous, and practise temperance.

   ### The second kind

   I want all the graces of the first kind as well as being balanced before all things. I do not want riches more than poverty, honour more than dishonour, longevity more than a short life, and so on. I want only to serve God and grow in grace.

The third kind

I desire the graces of both the first and the second kinds of humility. In addition I seek to know Christ more and become more the person that God's life within empowers me to be. I embrace the Christ-life which seeks only to be in relationship with God and in service of God's creative mission on earth. I know that the outcome of this choice will likely be as it was with Jesus Christ – poverty rather than riches, dishonour as opposed to honour – but I can choose nothing else for I am drawn to love and follow Christ.

2. Savour your prayer of day one.
3. Mark 4:1–9. From the boat, Jesus teaches the parable of the sower.
4. Savour your prayer of day three.

Sugar and salt

I am walking amongst the eucalypts
at Sugarloaf, looking for level ground.
I dig my chair into a wobbly place
shaded from the escalating heat.
Twigs and leaves crunch and crackle.
Bugs panic.

I am in the forest, and there is the lake.
Sunrise dreaming.
Kookaburra morning.

Inside the bald shore
the water blinks coy and often.
A salty spa on the eyes.

It could be Galilee.
Jesus in a boat
at the centre of a watery amphitheatre.
Crowds stirred by his words.
The smell of fish and sweat
in my nostrils.

I lean in to hear him.

5. Mark 5:24b–34. The healing of the woman with a haemorrhage.
6. Mark 5:24b–34. Read and ponder 'The last day'.

The last day

1.
The woman wrestled dreams
and woke with tranquillity and clarity.
One way or the other, today was her last,
the last day blood would drain
from her shrinking, painful body.
She dressed, gave thanks
she had no need
to go to the well today.

As every day, she opened her shutters,
took time to notice all
she had gathered.
Light played into her memories
friendship,
marriage,
man-touch,
washing and weaving.

She was ready.

She opened the latch,
heard the exhausted hinges.
She pulled her soft grey veil around her body,
and stepped onto the busy street,
stopping for a moment to feel
the sun sweep the contours of her face.

Past worrying about whispers
and blood-soaked clothes,
she must find strength to be
focused; every gesture and movement
conserved for one
momentous touch.

Season Two: Intimacy

2.
He was three deep.
Her heart recognised him,
and quickened in the seeing.

The shrill and lift of crowd
swamped her, left her dizzy
and light. Falling,

she reached out
the tips of her fingers,
feeling a wisp of warmth
from the hem of his garment.

He turned,
was strong against the moving crowd.

Who touched me?

Scared and sacred moment,
last moment of encounter
for which she dared not ask.

Longing words scarred in
blood and shame, emptied
from her –

I touched you.

You did, he said.

7. Savouring day.

Week Ten

Prayer for your spiritual desires
As the number of people following Jesus increases, so does the intensity of Jesus' prayer. There is a sense of increasing danger to Jesus as he stirs the crowd's faith and the officials' fear. Pray to increase your capacity to love Jesus and have compassion as he does.

Music
- Matt Hammitt, 'Trust' on the album *Every Falling Tear*. Sparrow records. 2011.

Prayer focus for the days of the week
1. John 6:1–15. Jesus feeds of the crowd.
2. Savour the prayer of day one.
3. Luke 5:17–26. Imaginative contemplation of the paraplegic lowered through the roof.
4. Savour the prayer of day three.

   Making myths to live by

   God is in no-man's-land
   where doors are shut
   and the creak of a disused hinge
   speaks a thousand invitations

5. Matthew 14:22–33. Jesus prays alone. Peter falters in faith.
6. Savour the prayer of day five.

Season Two: Intimacy

Via

when the shells of hard-edged things are peeled

and long-held images melt like snow
trickling down the hills of soft terrain

the muscles of moths cease to twitch
 wings fully open
ravens stop squawking

streams babble
 to hum

        to soundless wonder

there is nothing to think or say
nothing to do
nothing to thirst

7. Savouring day.

Week Eleven

Prayer for your spiritual desires

Again there is a sombre tone to some of the prayer texts this week. Listen to these texts through your present understanding of what concepts such as 'Satan', 'self-denial' and others might mean. Who might Elijah be in your life? What might 'son of man' mean? What is transfiguration? This is a week to hold in balance all that it might mean to know, love and follow Christ in your life in this 21st century. Pray that God will enlighten and console you in trust as you move forward.

Music
- Kimberly and Alberto Rivera, 'Breath of Life' on the album *Pneuma*. 2015.

Prayer focus for the days of the week

1. Matthew 8:23–27. Who is Jesus if he can calm the elements?

   Elementary

   No amount of self-talk or positive thinking
   can calm the anxiety roiling
   in the face of violence and terror.
   Only You calm these elements of my life.

2. Mark 8:27–33. *'Who do you say that I am?'*

   Who am I to be?

   I am an arguing Pharisee,
   witness to the multiplication of tiny resources.
   I have eaten bread in the desert,
   and forgotten.

This moment I do not recognise myself.
I am congested with thoughts
being seen and not heard.

I know what I am called to do
but who am I to be?
It is no small thing that You ask of me

but You give me a companion
to help when I am mute.

You touch my lips.
They feel refugee-stitched.
Your skin is warm and rough.
Your touch is gentle.

It would not matter what you said to me.
The sound of your voice even in the dark,
is tranquil in my soul.

I can only be who you say I am.

3. Mark 8:34—9:1. The cost of discipleship.
4. Mark 9:2–13. Jesus is transfigured.

White

Light blanches
        my seeing
burns through the senses. Dark
shadows give shape to you.

5. Mark 9:14–29. All things are possible with faith in God.

Union

At the moment you reach out to me
I lose my hands, my heart in you,
and become myself.

1. Mark 9:30–39. *Whoever is not against you is for you* (v. 39).
2. Savouring day. Choose to pray with some puzzling, confusing or consoling aspect of your prayer from this week.

Week Twelve

Prayer for your spiritual desires

Pray to relinquish all interior thoughts and feelings that would hinder your journey with Jesus. Pray for the grace to accompany Jesus through his most difficult times. Pray to be present to Jesus moment by moment.

Music

- Music Lab Collective, 'Writing's on the Wall' on the album *Peaceful Piano: A Journey to Complete Relaxation* CD 1. Decca. 2017.

Prayer focus for the days of the week

1. Matthew 10:1–16. Empowered and commissioned.
2. Luke 7:36–50. Anointing Jesus' feet.

   Lavender woman

   Simon, a Pharisee, a socialite, a colleague of Nicodemus, was curious about Jesus. He invited Jesus to share a meal, to have conversation and debate as Jews do. He expected Jesus (or anyone) to accept. And Jesus did. Simon welcomed him as one among many. They joked, told stories, became absorbed in competitive banter.

   Gold and purple embroidered cushions bordered the oiled table. At dinner Jesus reclined beside Simon. A woman, wearing russet and purple, entered the room. She knew the layout of the home, and had persuaded the servants to let her in. Jesus noticed her approach. Her eyes and cheeks were pink and wet.

   The woman removed her headscarf, loosened long braids and wiped her hair across Jesus' tanned and callused feet. He felt her gentle trembling hands, dismissed the guarded sniggers from the guests.

   Simon's eyes were wide beneath raised eyebrows, his jaw clenched, lips askew. He knocked over a cup. Red wine rolled across the wood, mingled with the tears falling onto Jesus' feet. Simon motioned to the servants.

The woman opened her bag, took from it a slender alabaster jar, and broke its neck. She poured the contents, massaging them into Jesus callused soles. Musk and lavender filled the room.

Again Jesus ignored the murmur coming from behind hands and handkerchiefs. He spoke to the woman. She stayed awhile.

And when she stood to leave, she smiled, seemed taller, left her headscarf on the floor.

3. John 2:13–22. Imaginative contemplation of this story in the Temple when the money changers are reprimanded by Jesus. You may want to read 'Uncomfortable love' in the additional material.

   Christ on the margins

   He upturns the table
   They upturn the soapbox
   He reads the raw underside
   They read the soapie side
   He speaks of love and vulnerability
   They speak of law and certainty
   He is crucified
   They are crassified

4. Savour the prayer of day three.
5. Luke 6:6–11. Sabbath healing of a disability. Imaginative contemplation.
6. Savour the prayer of day five. Read 'He sees and knows' in the additional material.
7. Savouring day. Where is your heart being drawn at present? Savour the consolations of the week's prayer. Notice any obstacles to your prayer.

Season Three: Compassion

Peter, you have companioned me all this time
but still you do not know love casts out fear.

Introduction

Of the four seasons of the spiritual exercises, the third, characterised by suffering love, has the potential to be the most profoundly affirming of humanity. It can unite a person to his or her own capacity to be loving, compassionate, fearful, hypocritical and self-seeking. To be reminded of positive potential seems easier than being reminded of its opposite. Why would anyone want to be reminded of their negative potential? It seems that God's love is greater than all our possible negatives. The retreatant seeks to share compassionately in the suffering of Jesus so as to become one with him through the mystery of suffering love.

In the garden of Gethsemane, Jesus begged *Abba*-God to spare him from what was about to happen. When it seemed that he would not be spared from the ordeal, Jesus rose from his place of agony, went to his friends, Peter, James and John, whom he had chosen to accompany him to the garden, and specifically asked Peter, *'Were you not able to be vigilant for one hour?'* (Mark 14:37; see also Matthew 26:40).

Gethsemane evening[1]

The disciples had eaten well at supper
(Jesus' appetite was poor)
They slept off their food and wine
lying around like drunken riff-raff
wherever they could find a bed
in Jerusalem.

His close friends were extra sleepy.
      It would seem
they had a premonition
Jesus was about to suffer
some sizeable interior conflict.
Sleep was avoidance.

---

1 See Mark 10:37; Matthew 20:21.

Jesus wanted encouragement.

His closest friends, Peter,
James and John, who argued
about seating arrangements
in the new Kingdom,
were chosen by Jesus
to be beside him at this time.

Now the cost was dawning –
Slumber was transformed

into nightmare.

In praying Season Three, turn to Jesus' *Abba* who, in human terms, appears to have abandoned Jesus at his darkest moments. As the retreatant finds a depth of compassion for Jesus in his suffering, the question is asked, 'Has *Abba* truly abandoned Jesus?'

Mass understood

Between the aisle
and the stooped father,
the man-boy shakes hands
off-beat
nods, shakes, nods
Let us pray
nods, stands, bows,
still
Two hands draw
two mind pistols
from holsters.
Replaced.
Drawn
the father mouths,
we are at mass.
Replaced.
Drawn,
half-cocked

man-boy smiles
displaced, he sits,
slumps, stiffens
his mind
bends
straightens
whispers to father,
words
no-one understands.

About your weekly visits to your spiritual director

Season Three is difficult to enter and sometimes difficult to leave. The companionship of your spiritual director will be invaluable, and yet this season often comes with fewer words and shorter sessions with your director. Seldom are the daily prayer periods shortened correspondingly.

Music

- Arvo Pärt (composer), 'Spiegel im Spiegel'. Dietmar Schwalke, Alexander Malter and Vladimir Spivakor (performers), on the album *Alina*, ECM Records. 2000.
- Audrey Assad, 'Even unto Death' on the album *Inheritance*. 2016.

Week One

As in the previous two seasons, you are encouraged to stay with the material which is helpful to your growth in relationship with the God of faith, hope and love. This might mean that one or two passages of scripture or one poem from the week will hold your interest. Receiving the graces does not depend on covering all the material.

Prayer for your spiritual desires

The grace for which you pray in this first week of Season Three is for union with Jesus in all he does as he prepares for his suffering. The grace is for a shared experience of suffering and the capacity to hold what is difficult to hold.

You will not be able to create this grace yourself, so the week will remind you of your dependence on Jesus' *Abba*, the God of Mystery. In God, all things are possible. This first week's prayer of Season Three asks you to accompany Jesus in the fulfilment of his ministry.

> **God's unconditional love**
>
> Love is an idea, a belief, a feeling
> confirmed by the beauty of the universe
> and moments of encounter with a person
> seemingly emptied of 'self'.
> But the possibility of unconditional love
> is a hope, a magnified window
>
> through which one gazes on another reality,
> buoyed by the experience
> of logic and other larger things
>
> especially that God is Love.

Music
- Patrick Doyle, 'Please Forgive Me' (Thor's Soundtrack), on the album *Wah*-Wah (Original Motion Picture Soundtrack). 2005.

Season Two: Intimacy

Prayer focus for the days of the week

1. Luke 22:1–13. Imaginative contemplation on the plans and actions of Judas, the financier. Preparations for the Supper.

   Judas in spring

   Judas, it is spring.
   Your life is sprouting thorns.
   It would be better
   had you not been watered.

2. Savour the prayer of day one. You might also read 'Twenty-four Hours' in the additional material.
3. Luke 22:14–20. The narrative of the final supper in which Jesus shares food and drink with his friends. Jesus shares himself with all of us.

   Holy-there

   When called,
   she tried to love more,
   and this love – saying yes
   to self-emptiness –
   was the cross
   she wished would pass her by.

   So they gathered by his side
   embraced in a tide of helplessness.
   The one who loved the most
   leaned to his breast, was his host
   and blessing. She knew
   it was her privileged holy-there –

   to be there in prayer.

4. Savour the prayer of day three.
5. John 13:1–20. Jesus washes the feet of his friends.
6. Savour the prayer of day five. Imaginative contemplation. Read 'Serious Song' and 'God puzzles with me' in the additional material.

7. Savour the week's prayer.

   Communion of saints

   I ponder the fields of weeds and wheat,
   and disperse, like seeds,
   my guilt and anger, also love,
   across the spread of ancestors and progeny.
   In the sowing and the harvest,
   I share my nourishment with you.
   We are bread.

Week Two

Prayer for your spiritual desires

In Season Three, it is easy to become distracted by your own suffering or shortcomings. The graces of the season are compassion with Jesus as he suffers and the embodiment of his self-giving love. Pray for the grace that you might stay with him in all the experiences of his passion. Can you stay awake with him, for him? Can you allow yourself to feel the sorrow of what your friend Jesus is enduring?

Music
- Kathleen Claire, 'Sometimes' on the album *Lyrics of a Woman*. 2011.

Prayer focus for the days of the week

1. Matthew 26:30–56. The narrative of Jesus from the upper room to the garden of Gethsemane. Jesus' agony and conversation with *Abba*.

   Words to Peter

   Put your bloodied sword back in the scabbard
   and your impetuous temper along with it.
   Peter, you have companioned me all this time
   but still you do not know love casts out fear
   before fear justifies itself and turns to violence.

   The night has fallen and so shall you. Three times my friend,
   you will deny me. You will by your word.

   Do not cling to me but let the present moment
   be. I have said 'yes'. I must have your 'yes',
   at least for now, at the very least.

2. Savour part of the prayer of day one.

Integrity

Integrity is costly.
There are no bonds
and little interest.

3. John 18:12–27. Jesus is taken to Annas. Peter denies Jesus. Jesus is assaulted.

Maple meditation

Rays of light touched the maple leaf,
and I am sure it trembled

as if a breeze came down from heaven
to move its stillness from complacency.

And in the silence, the leaf shimmered,
and every leaf on every branch shone with it.

I drew back – saw the leaf as a hand
so vast that all things known were held in it.

Something made me stay. I think someone –
the presence, I feared, had captivated me.

I watched the leaf fall as one falls in love
and feels there is no choice,

as one who comes to know *I will*
are the only words to feel.

I will let you undo my will
and take me where you want to go.

4. Savour your prayer of a previous day.
5. Mark 14:53–72. Jesus goes before the Sanhedrin. He is tortured.

Laying hands

On them, Jesus laid hands
holy hands
healing hands
moving hands
working hands
open hands

Do not turn them away.

On him they laid hands
stained hands
brutal hands
arresting hands
clenched hands

We turn away.

6. Savour the prayer of day five.
7. Savouring day. Savour the week of prayer.

Week Three

Prayer for your spiritual desires

Continue to pray for the grace of deep awareness of what Jesus is suffering. Allow your own life experience to help you to be compassionate for Jesus as he suffers. You have a human-divine nature as Jesus does, and therefore have the capacity to be a friend to Jesus. Be merciful to yourself for failed friendships and turn towards Jesus. Now is the time to consider what kind of friendship you can offer him.

Music

- Taizé Community Choir, 'Stay with me' on the album *Songs of Taizé: O Lord Hear My Prayer* and *My Soul is at Rest*. Volume One. 2008.

Prayer focus for the days of the week

1. Matthew 27:1-2; 11-14. Jesus before Pilate.

   Unnamed poem

   I have sat beside you
   bathed and caressed you
   lover of my light and darkness
    I will hold you
    respect you
   gentle your every wish
   as you draw near and nearer
   to the One you have known
   and not known.

         Part of me
   ripped away   My heart gapes

   I am hollow and heavy
   with absence   I reach out
   as if to catch the holon
   you forgot

Season Three: Compassion

    to leave behind
    My senses, confused
    in the fragrant memory,
    the touch and tenderness of first love

2. Savour the prayer of day one.
3. Luke 23:5 –12. Jesus meets Herod.
4. Savour your prayer of day three.
5. Matthew 27:15–26 Jesus is before Pilate again. The crowd is given the choice of whether to release Barabbas or Jesus.

Slow

    It was only when I dared to see
    that I was she
    standing in a street of passers-by,

    only then after I had walked on,
    and turned back
    to find she was gone,

    only later that day
    when I tried
    to hold her shadows
    on a page

    in the blackest hues of red and blue
    inside the grey pearl, her face,
    my heart,

    when the depth of her stillness,
    the suffering numbed in her
      stuck lips

    in an arc of blood,

    my fingers touching
    the image before me

    smudging the paper with sorrow,

    only then did I see
    the face of Christ.

6. Savour your prayer of day five.
7. Savouring day. Which prayer this week has brought you closer to Jesus? Which prayer has brought the greatest distractions? Pray for the grace of Season Three, compassion.

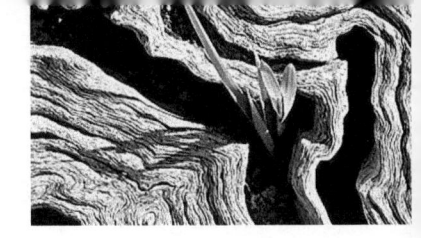

Week Four

Prayer for your spiritual desires
Ask God for the grace to stay compassionately with Jesus each day this week.

Music
- Ólafur Arnalds, 'Pú ert Jördin' on the album *Living Room Songs*. 2011.
1. Matthew 27:26–32. Jesus is scourged and begins the walk to Calvary.

   Forging the only path

   Life is striped
   like the lashes on Jesus' body
   and the tiger snake the man encountered,
   coiled beside a track forged through
   native grass in Yarra Bend Park.

   He stood for a moment or millions of years,
   slipping on a knife edge
   and wanting to go forward
   even if the knife cut open his heart.

   And what rose up was his reptilian brain
   claiming the territory carefully

   while the snake returned to solitude,
   and he walked on alone
   past the deadly myth
   into mystery.

2. Savour the prayer of day one, or read the poem 'Calvary' in the additional material.
3. Matthew 27:33–38. Jesus is stripped and crucified. Two criminals are crucified with him, one on either side.
4. Matthew 27:39–47. Jesus feels abandoned by *Abba*.

5. Pray your heart is big enough to stay with Jesus. Reflect on the poem 'Holding him'.

   Holding him

   There is nothing romantic
   about bones and barely-breath.

   Straight from the heart,
   her arms are firm around him –
   (once they wouldn't have made it).
   Now he is vulnerable and trusting.
   The best he ever was.
   The weight of him gone.

   His daughters
   in swift and calculated manoeuvres
   make the bed comfortable.
   He cannot sit
   without slipping to the floor.
   He splashes words.
   Letters land anywhere.
   The sisters pick them up.

   She holds him closely.
   His rough grey cheek near hers.
   All the saliva spent.
        Anger
   dissipated. He helps on one weak leg.

        Trembling
   she finds it possible to give
   her best. It is enough.
   These few seconds.

6. Pray to integrate your graces into your daily life.

Season Three: Compassion

Ours

There are no shoes, no walls or boundaries.
Hot, black feet stand equally
on the ashen face of earth,
where mountain ash last week
made worship easy. Today

spindly, charcoal arms reach
through umber air to a mute sky.
While all looked well in Doncaster,
thirty minutes north east,
a fire gulped with legion tongues,

feather and fur, possessions
and possessor. It mocked,
spitting embers four kilometres down wind,
random as the massacre of Hoddle Street.
There was nothing to be done but

bare their souls
and fear the ground of earth and urn,
listen to its lone and crackling voice and
the dulling cry from somewhere
in hot breathless smoke. Five persons huddled

in the front of a ute, disconnected
from everything that doesn't matter.
My God, this country holds the spirit of those
who stand in ash and flood –
who feel chaos draw the deep-shared moan.

7. Savouring day.

Week Five

Prayer for your spiritual desires
Pray for compassion for all the characters in the narrative this week. Pray for whatever grace you need.

Music
- Ólafur Arnalds, 'Ágúst' on the album *Living Room Songs*. 2011.

Prayer focus for the days of the week
1. Luke 23:33–34. *Father forgive them.* The narrative of the good thief.
2. Savour the prayer of day one.
3. Pray with 'Mary's soliloquy'.

> **Mary's soliloquy**
> *Jesus wept* (John 11:35).
>
> Slumped at the foot of our cross
> silently, consciously praying for courage
> to raise my eyes to you. And when it comes,
> I see you drift in and out of consciousness.
> The quiet pauses lengthen.
> I refuse to drink while you thirst.
>
> I mourned a gentler goodbye –
> some discussion about your wishes,
> but now, such things are meaningless.
>
> The soldiers have threatened me.
> I refuse to leave.
> I would rather be on that cross.
>
> John has offered his hand to me.
> but I want no-one but you.
>
> *How can this be?* I ask again.
> *Will you come to me in my dreams?*

Jesus, you are silent.
I wait for your next frail breath.
It is not happening. It does not happen.
I am empty. I remember to breathe
when I would rather not.

4. John 19:25–30. Jesus dies.

   Surrender

   Trampled, empty
   lungs folded and rolled.

   There is only silence
   still as death.
   Silence weeping,
   seeping from a tear
   in some nameless organ.

   I look upon myself
   in deepest recognition. Perhaps
   words I cannot find exist.

   I see
   I am

   fully myself, fully broken
   fully Christ.

5. John 19:31–42. Jesus is taken down from the cross.
6. Savour your prayer of days four or five.

Body of Christ

> Go into the bare chapel.
> On the wall you will see a
> crucifix,
> cold and uncompanioned.
> Jesus hangs peeling,
> plaster broken off one leg,
> exposing a rod,
> the rusty interior –
> bare.

Go bare into the chapel.

7. Savouring day.

Week Six

Jesus is in the tomb. This is a time to reflect on the whole journey of Jesus' life. What might it have been like for the friends of Jesus to gather at his wake, to reflect on their experiences, to wonder, to be disappointed, to hope still? Which friend of Jesus has been a companion for you throughout this journey of the seasons? Which companion has shared in your joys and sorrows? With whom have you felt the greatest empathy and the greatest compassion?

Scriptures which assisted the friends of Jesus might also be helpful to you:

Genesis 1:1–2.4; 22:1–18
Exodus 14:15—15.1
Isaiah 54:5–14; 55:1–11
Baruch 3:9–15; 3:32—4:4
Ezekiel 36:16–28

    Enough

    The fog hid sky and earth.
    Its consonance with my soul
    drew me to wonder –
    what cannot be seen?
    I long to see the marsh wren
    which whistles in the reeds.
    Today I sit beside you,
    the fog and reeds between us.

Season Four: Joyful Passion

You and I see shadows
stirring and shaping
character and plot

Introduction

After giving his pilgrims the first three seasons of the *Spiritual Exercises*, Ignatius often gave them the fourth season to pray on their pilgrimage home. It was appropriate to do so, as Season Four seeks to connect a person to joy in the Mystery of God through all creation.

The prayer material in the text of this season, however, presumes the continuation of conversations with your spiritual director.

> **Co-creating**
>
> Hunting and gathering
> in sacred spaces
> watching, reading
> the narrative.
>
> I hear whispering syllables
> through my silenced self,
> feel breath thaw my tongue,
> let it move me.
>
> You bare your soul,
> amplify the fluttering
> of first words –
>
> wings escaping walls
> of a once-safe cocoon.
>
> Wise and gentle one,
> you have coaxed me to be grateful
> for the sinking day,
> for sounds bringing peace to the night,
> and for the first sight of morning dew.
>
> Now, you and I see shadows,
> stirring and shaping
> character and plot,
> awaiting the new.

About joy

The quality and character of joy in Season Four is not always flamboyant and extroverted. Joy can be stillness and quietude in humble awe. Pray for the grace to find the joy which is uniquely yours. If the grace of risen joy does not come to you during the fourth season, pray that the grace will come at a later stage. It will come perhaps when you least expect it.

Serious joy

You know about serious joy
deep in the chambers of the heart.
It can't be ignored.
It is a piece of God's own heart
thrown to you with dart precision.

And when it pierces your heart,
God sings the sound
consoling you, filling you

as if with an angel's soft sigh.
Rilke says a smile goes somewhere.
I imagine it touching the atmosphere –
its pink helium making the world
lighter, more buoyant,
spinning the universe.

Music
\#   Lisa Kelly, 'The Deer's Cry' on the album *Lisa*. Celtic Woman Presents: Lisa, 2006.

Contemplatio
The *Contemplatio* is Ignatius' meditation which helps the retreatant to learn

to love like God. It has four reflective themes:

- Gifts of life, faith and relationships
- God's self-giving in Christ
- God's co-creative presence with us
- Infinite Love.

Suscipe

The following prayer, based on Ignatius' ***Suscipe*** (Latin, 'receive'), is suggested to accompany you throughout Season Four.

Holding

Palms tremble
lifting before You

the embodied fruit
of my labour

I know
my offering

total
unblemished

comes from You
returns to You

Take
Receive
all

An English version of the Spanish **Suscipe** *prayer of Ignatius* [1]

Take and receive

God, take and receive all my liberty, my memory, my understanding, and my entire will, all that I have and possess. You have given all to me. To You, I return it. All is Yours, dispose of it wholly according to Your holy desires. Give me Your love and grace, for this is sufficient for me.

---

1 Loyola Press. A Jesuit Ministry, *Suscipe. St Ignatius of Loyola*, 2019.

Week One

Prayer for your spiritual desires

The grace for which you pray in Season Four is to rejoice with Jesus Christ in his joy and to embody Christ in the world. This joy celebrates the overcoming of death by creation and renewal. You have shared in Jesus' suffering, and now you can share in his joy. The two sides of the mystery are not divisible. As is often said, we can only know the heights of joy if we have experienced the depths of suffering. In Season Four, can you notice opportunities for joy and find ways to nurture a sense of joy in your life?

Although the scriptures and Church tradition do not enshrine the belief that Mary the mother of Jesus was the first person to encounter the risen Jesus, it seems obvious to Ignatius that this was true. On the first day of Season Four, you are offered the possibility of praying with this encounter. You might also like to refer to the resurrection narrative in Luke 24.

Music

- Pink (Alecia Moore) and Happy Feet Chorus, 'Bridge of Light' (Single) from the film *Happy Feet 2*. Published by EMI Blackwood Music, Inc., obo itself and Pink Inside Publishing (BMI), Sony ATV Sounds LLC, Turtle Victory (SESAC). Produced by Billy Mann for the Well Ltd. 2011.

Prayer focus for the days of the week

1. Song of Songs 2:8–14. Winter is past. 'You are my son, my love, my life.'[1]

    Imagine the meeting between Jesus Christ and his mother Mary. Your imaginative contemplation might include the location where they meet, the dynamic between them, the words spoken and unspoken, onlookers (such as yourself), your thoughts and feelings about this encounter.

2. Finding Christ in our loved ones. Read 'Love letter after Skype' in the additional material.

---

[1] Marburg, *An Ordinary Woman*, p. 84.

3. Mark 16:1–11. Imaginative contemplation of Jesus appearing to Mary Magdalene outside the tomb.
4. 'The Magdalene sequence'.

The Magdalene sequence

1
Perfect number – seven –
a legion of devils banished.

Mary, you knew Beelzebub
babbling *Holy One of God
Son of the Most High.*

You grew to know
the Most Lowly One, and one
by one, the cowering devils left.

2
For generations you were
a shamed
unholy secret,
silenced.

They said you bedded plenty –
pride, lust and vanity
and the worst – self-abasement,
but poor or whore or purple lady[2],
your words remain anointed.

We hear the Spirit speak
long before saints were Saints
and Peter was pope.

If they had known,
they would have asked you
to exorcise their demons.

---
2 Purple signifies wealth; purple dye for the clothing of wealthy people.

3

You enter and break convention at the table –
pour oil on his honoured head.

You cannot stop your tears mingling
with grace undone –
ointment spilt from the alabaster jar.

He lets your supple hands stroke
his robust veins, his callused soles.
He ignores the sins you tell.
Each kiss upon his feet transforms each sin.

You blot extravagance with your hair
and lavish love hangs fragrant in the air,

The host is confused.

4

You have known the ways of purple
and the cross.

The stony grief on which you kneel is hard.
Embalmed in tears, you are
too numb to rise.

5

Why do you weep, Mary?
Rabbouni raises you.
His arms hold all that you can be.

Go tell them.

6

No more will you carry balms and spice
to anoint what is dead.
Death cannot rise. It gives rise.

7

Disciples of the mind hear nonsense
when you tell them;
affection for the dead makes no sense.
But non-sense wells within the hopeful few.

> 8
> Mary, any woman,
> welcomed at the table,
> we come to share your tears.
> We take your hands
> in our extravagant embrace.
> We anoint Christ in anyone.
>
> 9
> We honour your gospel.

5. Savour prayers from previous days. Read 'Mary's grace' in the additional material.
6. Luke 24:9–12; 34. Peter runs to the tomb.
7. Savouring day. Read *Suscipe* and 'Holding'.

Week Two

Prayer for your spiritual desires

Take and receive who I am

Receive only who I am,
all that you have given me,
the seeds sown
in my mind, choices, desires.

And if you should receive who I am not,
transform by your great love these affected parts
into the beauty of your grace.
And I will recognise myself
as your sufficient delight.

Music
- 'Bird Song: Songs of Nature for Wellbeing' on the album *Spirit of Meditation*. Meditation Music Guru. 2013.

Prayer focus for the days of the week
1. John 20:16–33. The absence of Thomas as the disciples gather. Jesus visits and offers peace.
2. John 16:16–33. Joy emerges from sorrow.
3. Savour your prayer of day one or day two.
4. You are encouraged to pray your own *Contemplatio* which is the 'Contemplation for Learning to Love Like God' [231-237]. See the general notes in the introduction to Season Four, above. The following poem is an example of the content of the *Contemplatio*.

Contemplatio

I pray to love like God
And I remember –

Jelly-orange sun at Cable Beach
Stately Mountain Ash along the Black Spur
Vineyards painting the Yarra Valley autumn
Warm hands testing an open fire
Eye to eye with a newborn child
Lungs filled with the breath of God
A comic poet juggling words.

Some things prop me up a little
and others make me fly.

5. Luke 24:13–35. Two friends on the road to Emmaus.

Afire

On the road to Emmaus,
as Cleopas and I walked,
our voices were flat and bare-breath.
Our teacher and friend
had gone from us.

But there was something
about the stranger who joined us,
something about his voice
that tapped into our desire,
his words that stirred our belief,
quelled our grief.

And over the meal, we remembered
our hearts burned
as he talked on the way.

Our slow hospitality
welcomed him, and
we settled

beside the fire
burning between us.

6. Savouring day. 'Take and receive who I am.'
7. What part of the *Contemplatio* is drawing you? Can you begin to write your own contemplation as you learn to love like God?

Week Three

joy
is gift
fire wrapping
a log soft smoky
ringlets, ribbon-
stories billowing
warming

Prayer for your spiritual desires
Continue to pray to know and experience the joy of Christ alive in your heart.

Music
- Becky Williams, 'Amazing Day' on the album *The Hero's Journey*. 2003.

Prayer focus for the days of the week
1. 1 Corinthians 12:14–26. We are one body.
2. John 20:24–29. Thomas encounters the risen Jesus.
3. Psalm 100. *Contemplatio.* Learning to love like God.
4. Matthew 18:19–20. Jesus promises to be with us.
5. John 21:1–17. The fishing trip followed by a barbecue on the shores of Lake Tiberius.
6. Responding to call contemplation of the poem 'Into the deep'.

Into the deep

When I am clean finished –
everything diminished –
I put my hands into the night,
roll up the last hope like a burial cloth

at the end of the worst day.
Emptiness floods and falls like the tides.
And I am on my knees suddenly
Soaked in splashing moonlight.

I feel the unmistakable tremble:

Roll up your sleeves,
bare your hands to the light,
paddle your heart into the deep.
Fish are clamouring at the boat,
ready to die for freedom.

7. Savouring prayer. 1 Corinthians 12:14–26

Interpretive paraphrase of 1 Corinthians 12:14–26

The person is not made up of one part but many. Now if imagination should say, *because I am not hands-on, I do not belong to the person*, it would not, for that reason, stop being part of the person. And if spirituality should say, *because I am not visible, tangible, measurable, I do not belong to the person*, it would not, for that reason, stop being part of the person. If the whole person were affectivity, where would be the sense of the spirit? If the whole self were sexuality, where would be the intellect? But in fact God has placed the dimensions within the person, every one of them, just as they are. Personal spirituality cannot say to sexuality, 'I don't need you!' And genitality cannot say to spirituality, 'I don't need you!' Parts of the body that seem vulnerable are indispensable, and the parts that we think shameful are honourable. And the parts that are hidden are known and treated with respect, and the parts that are esteemed are a gift to all other parts. But God has put the body together, giving greater honour to the parts that lacked it, so that there should be no division in the body, but that its parts should have equal concern for each other. If one part suffers, every part suffers with it; if one part is honoured, every part rejoices with it. There are many parts, but one person, one body, and each part is intimate with each other part. If we are to think that we are independent, we are all the more dependent, for we are stumbling in our lack of understanding. We are the cosmos; we are our universe; we are the stars and sun and moon; we are the earth, our forebears and our progeny. We are each other.

Week Four

You are near the end of *Grace upon Grace: Savouring the Spiritual Exercises through the Arts*. Your experience of the graces of these exercises are specific to you. Are you wondering what these graces will mean to you and your lifestyle?

Prayer for your spiritual desires

The grace for which you might pray this week is for gratefulness for yourself, your journey and for all that fills your life. You might ask for a deep desire to incarnate your consolations. This is the desire to live from the consoling grace of friendship with Jesus. The *Suscipe* prayer, alongside the Principle and Foundation of the *Spiritual Exercises*, might help you again this week and into the future.

Music

- The Wailin' Jennys, 'One Voice' on the album *The Wailin' Jennys: Live at the Mauch Chunk Opera House*. 2009.
- Lorraine Hess, 'Take O Lord and Receive' on the album *As I Pray*. 2015.

Prayer focus for the days of the week

1. Matthew 28:16–20. Commissioning the friends of Jesus.

    Be the poem

    Open yourself
    and the white page

    the face
    empty of agenda

    flawless face
    that does not rise up
    or judge

    the easy to kiss face
    wooed by pen and ink

shaping truth

the mirrored face
reading your mind
feeling your hand

showing your heart

2. The *Contemplatio*. Finish writing the contemplation which you began on day seven of Season Four, week two. Create a mandala in response to your contemplation of creation and God with us.
3. 1 John 4:7–21. God is love.
4. Paraphrase of the 'Principle and Foundation' [23] below and *Suscipe*.

Principle and Foundation

I am created to reflect God. I am intended to bring beauty and fullness to all that God creates me to be and empowers me to do. God created me out of love, for love. Only in love can God's full imagination be realised. Only in full communion with God can all persons and all reality know wholeness.

God's world has become disordered through unconscious and conscious acts, rejecting full knowledge and wisdom. Disorder is not the flux or polarities of everyday dynamics but rather a failure to recognise and act in accordance with the love of God instilled in our hearts. This love creates in me desires to participate in my life-world through my personal, centring dynamic. It enables me to find from the choices available to me that which will empower or disempower my life. What reason would I ever have to choose to be disempowered? Why would I ever choose to disconnect myself from my life source?

5. Acts 1:3; 1 Corinthians 15:6–8. The apparitions of Jesus.
6. Acts 9:1–22; Acts 22:1–15. Paul's revelation.
7. Savouring day.

Other possible scriptures
Jeremiah 31:1–20.
Colossians 3:5–17.
Romans 8:3–39.

Week Five

The immediate men and women friends of Jesus and those in the early Christian communities (Acts 1:14) were challenged to embody their consolations, and were empowered to overcome the obstacles of preaching a new way of living as Jews and Gentiles.

In our contemporary world, the challenges have been equally great from within and outside the traditional churches. This is the week to pray for the anointing of women and men to the companionship of empowerment that is affirmed and enacted in Jesus Christ.

> **Beyond division**
>
> They have come
> with discerning hearts
> open to discuss issues from decades
> of turbulence among the people of God.
> They know to listen to the spirit
> wanting only what builds love –
>
> One hour of silence each day –
> And the sharing begins.
> The people will gather for as long as it takes.
> Every nation, proud and humble,
> fills the space with warmth and daring.
>
> Hope is rising, expanding
> the hearts of every woman, every man.

Prayer for your spiritual desires

This week, pray to deepen your joy in Christ so that you might fulfil the call to journey and co-create with God in your authentic calling.

Music
- Karl Jenkins, 'Benedictus' on the album *The Armed Man – A Mass for Peace*. EMI. 2010.

Prayer focus for the days of the week
1. Acts 1:1–12. Ephesians 4:7–16. Testimony of Jesus' disciples.
2. Luke 24:50–53. The Ascension of Jesus Christ.
3. Acts 2:1–8. Pentecost.
4. Acts 21:1–21. Your sons and daughters shall prophesy.
5. Acts 16:13–14; Acts 17:4, 12 and 34. The women. In what ways do you identify with the women?
6. Romans 8:18–27. Creation will be set free.
7. Ephesians 3:14–21. Strength and empowerment in your inner self.

Principle and foundation

There is nothing in this galaxy
or the universe beyond,
nothing on the face of this planet
or underneath to its depth,
that cannot help each one and all
to respond to Love's call to communion.

There is no hierarchy of goods
in abundance or lack.

In any moment, the heart of a person hears
what gives life, and what draws life away,
what elicits love or hate,
what creates and impassions,
what extinguishes hope,
and which decisions loosen the heart
to love, to cry, to give,
to stand in awe before all that is.

There is No End to Grace

The following questions are suggested to help you transition from praying the spiritual exercises to your prayer in everyday life. They are also a tool for you to reflect on your experience of the full spiritual exercises.

Preparation Days

1. Do you recall what sparked your interest in praying the full *Spiritual Exercises* of Saint Ignatius? What expectations did you have before you began?
2. How would you characterise your relationship with Divine Mystery at the beginning of the spiritual exercises?
3. Was there some specific interest in praying the exercises using a creative approach?
4. Did you know your spiritual director prior to the commencement of the spiritual exercises? If so, what helped /hindered you? What helped you to trust your director?
5. Did you pray using the arts? Poetry? Dance/movement? Journal writing? Drawing/painting? Music? Other? How did the arts help you in your prayer of the spiritual exercises?
6. Did the natural environment feature much as you began the spiritual exercises?
7. How did you experience praying with scripture in the preparation period?

Season One: Love

8. How did the Preparation Days help your disposition towards the prayer of Season One: Love?
9. What was your image of God at this point in the spiritual exercises?
10. What grace(s) did you receive in Season One?
11. Did anything surprise you in Season One?
12. What did you value about any particular prayer/meditation/contemplation?

13. What was your view of sin before praying Season One? What changed in your understanding?
14. Did you experience a deep sense of God as Divine Love? Any other sense of God?
15. Did you stay long enough in Season One? Would you have liked this season to be shorter or longer? Why is that?

Season Two: Intimacy

16. Were you ready to begin Season Two: Intimacy? How were you helped to transition from Season One to Season Two?
17. In what ways did you benefit from praying the meditations of Season Two?
    α. The Incarnation
    β. The Infancy narratives
    χ. Two Values
    δ. Three Couples
    ε. Three Kinds of Humility
18. Season Two is long. How did you manage the length?
19. What was the main grace for you in Season Two?
20. Were you able to discover some characteristics of Jesus which were previously unrecognised by you?
21. Do you recall the mood of the exercises as you were finishing Season Two? Did you want to move on to Season Three? Why?

Season Three: Compassion

22. How did you experience Jesus' suffering in Season Three?
23. Were you able to stay with him as he suffered on the cross?
24. What kinds of suffering are difficult for you to bear?
25. How have you been accompanied in your own suffering?
26. What grace is still alive to you as you recall Season Three?
27. How were you graced by the 'tomb day'?

Season Four: Joyful Passion

28. At the end of Season Three, were you ready to move on to the resurrection narratives?
29. What important grace were you given in Season Four?
30. Did any person in these narratives become alive to you in a new way? In what way?
31. Have you deepened your experience of Christ alive within you? How is that for you?

General Questions

32. Were there any people from the scriptures who have left a lasting impression on you?
33. Did any of Jesus' family, friends or disciples become important for you as you journeyed through the spiritual exercises?
34. Which season of the prayer was the most cathartic for you?
35. How would you characterise your relationship with Divine Mystery at the end of the spiritual exercises?
36. What is your image of God now?
37. What did you learn about yourself from the experience of the spiritual exercises?
38. What graces are still with you as you re-orientate yourself to prayer without the spiritual exercises?
39. Do you need a prayer frame to help you sustain your prayer life? What kind of frame would be helpful?
40. What is your deepest desire as you finish the spiritual exercises?
41. Did you receive what you had hoped for as you began the exercises?
42. How might you live from the graces given during this sacred retreat?

Additional material

Preparation Days

Prodigal Sequence

Sage sister

Father is mostly wise
but since my brother left,
He speaks hope and grief
in the same sentence.

Mother holds her silence.

My impetuous brother
left months ago
pockets full.

I have sewn a robe for him.
It gathers dust.

I want him home.

What disgrace might draw him back?

Forever mother

Did I give him too much?
      Too little?

He is naïve.

He will be shocked
when the customs' officials
demand taxes for his travels.

He will gamble and lose,
find solace in a whore.

They say my husband is a sage,

    … but I have lost my son.

I remember
his soft small hands in mine,
and how he pulled me
towards the pond
to see the ducklings file
after mother.

Ambivalent brother

The best part of me
is glad he has had his way.
He will learn as children,
through experience.

The worst part of me
hopes he never comes back.

Prodigal father

I have let go.

Of course I want him home.
He will tell his story
in his charismatic way.

In a dream

    I know his shadow
    long across the yellow field.

    He comes,

and I am there
running towards him
not nearly fast enough.

My hands around him hold his bony frame.

I tell him nothing can change
the love I have for him.

Dreaming son

In a winter field, ragged and sole-torn,
I slip over and again.
The organic smell closes in

the pigpen. I grasp the last sludgy scraps,
as if bread and wine.

I am intoxicated by remorse. At night
I dream I am icy cold.

> My father runs to me,
> remembering me
> when I was in my senses.
> He hugs me
> as a father can.

By day, I smell the field
soft yellow-lit. Ready for harvest.
Rye chafes my throat.
I am cramped with hunger.
Rogue tears roll from heart to eyes.
My life is upside down.

I am deeply in the process of birth,
the crying place,
shivering until breast held,
shawled and honoured.

Season One: Love

Auntie Mary

I love this woman I never met.
Mary who brought life to dad.
She was single, stood-up,
had a baby – Dolly,
the 'orphan' she raised.
Silent shame. Stoning.

When grandma died,
Mary was a stand-in,
stood-up mother
to my father
There was no shame in that.

I met Mary's Dolly. She looked like Dad.
I loved her resonant voice, sincere smile.
She seemed strong and gentle all at once.
'Doll' corresponded with Dad.
She was Mary to him.
Enunciating. Annunciating.
I am drawn to Marys.

Jesus and Gandhi

In sturdy, peaceful stride
side by side, silent
      in their truth,

Jesus and Gandhi stop suddenly
to say to the aggressors,
      Don't shoot.

He is my friend.
Don't take him away.

He loves you – in truth.
They crucified Jesus; shot Gandhi,
still steeped in rhetoric
'   What is truth?'

There is no answer for those
who seek the deprived way

agreeing with values
unchallenged, closed
to truth

Can you imagine a fulcrum at balance?
The moment of relinquishment
where knowing and not knowing are
indistinguishable truth and lie;

one moment of open perception
where all things are equal
– save the one thing –
which leads to God.

Follow Jesus and Gandhi.
          Watch where they go.

Becoming conscious

I do believe
we are in a process
of becoming conscious.
It can permit chaos.

To think disturbance is abnormal
is to imagine a static world
where we are unmoved.

Order includes enough disturbance
to make the world rotate,
to sustain a heart-beat,
to allow rain and sunshine
and condensation in between.

Disorder is a crazy calm,
satisfaction with the status quo,
peace at any price.

Disorder is the refusal to live
between loss and gain,
to reject growth
and growing consciousness.

Disorder is the refusal
to accept love
while we are yet confused
and attached to questions
about Mystery,
questions emerging
from a literal awareness and
those refusing to engage with a world
in the process of becoming conscious.

Disorder is a fear that my world
will be different in the morning.

Season Two: Intimacy

Winter's wait

Slowly
rainbow droplets cling to one another
as if life depends on it.

Chill spreads, bridging gaps
as blossom swell on plum trees.

In half-light, water birds fluff their feathers,
nestle closely, freeze
their song in the growing ice

and the world turns blue   waiting.

Senses

Travel has been slow.
Darkness has come early.
Mary and Joseph wait in the census line
with a wry smile for tomorrow –
the tally will be outdated!
But consolation has come to them.
Their expectations have landed them in an animal shelter,
through the kindness of a householder.

And he is born and she is drawn outside herself.
The child is visible, palpable and frail.
Why is she surprised that her baby is a boy?

She sleeps and wakes, watches the baby looking out,
as the eyelids of the world open. There are
flashes of light this starry night,
about which they wonder.
Words are redundant.

Distant voices slowly strengthen
and then there is a knock at the door.
The quirky sages are welcomed
though the householder is perplexed.
Shrewd shepherds, whose toil it is to care
for lambing ewes and bleating sheep, come.
Come in. Strangers are not strange to a baby.
Life is all brand new.
He might not know again what
he knows now. For a moment

the voice of Mary soothes his hunger.
He settles with her smell and touch, her closeness.
She cannot imagine herself apart from him.

Dreaming a grace

I imagine a place with a fire,
people gathering
sharing food and conversation
deep desires,
the way things can be across the globe at this time
when structures are imploding
and a new consciousness of God in all things, even pain, is
emerging –

and there is no competition,
no striving to be or do anything –

I imagine listening and awakening, and holding
as precious each other
and each other's gifts and each other's dreams,
inviting each other to speak,
to tell stories, create myths,
to challenge and be challenged by the arts,
say what can only be spoken in airy spaces,
sifting what stifles and limits vision
from what expands love and kindness.

I imagine insight and discernment,
holy decisions and implementation.
I imagine shared prayer,
uplifting grace
and love that doesn't know stinginess
or maintaining the way things have been.
I imagine leadership that enables,
recedes from its ego, from the disabling
power of self-doubt.

I imagine a ritual of reclaiming, reshaping
a communion of souls.
I see faces and clear eyes
lifted to the heaven
in each other

I imagine a quiet interior *yes,*
a buoyant *yes* that can weather the storms

that try to enclose us or drown God's feet in us.

I imagine daring and courage
until they are no longer such.

I imagine the *yes* of Jesus
tipping tables and healing hearts,
the yes-disposition to all things God
that took him to Gethsemane.

I imagine
post-resurrection people,
Pentecost people
living the unquenchable flame.

I wonder what you imagine.

The Marriage feast

Family and friends looked forward to John and Esther's wedding. Today is the wedding day. Guests dance and sing. They tell stories about the couple, about their love; a marriage written in their hearts. The meal is about to be served. The air is heavily spiced.

Mary, the mother of Jesus frowns and whispers, *They have no wine.*

Why worry? Jesus says. *John and Esther aren't worried.*

In her heart Mary knows that having no wine is an embarrassment to the parents and guests. Wine is the symbol of joy and hospitality. It brings warmth and celebration. And there is none left!

Jesus walks outside. The music gives way to the bleating sheep and mooing cattle. He notices the moist spring air and the scent of cut grass. A lone untidy grapevine grows beside an old fence. He picks an immature grape and squeezes it between his fingers. The pungent smell makes him feel sad.

He ponders how he loves the wedding couple and how they had asked him to propose the toast during the wedding feast. He had wondered what he would say that might add to the couple's perfect day.

He rehearses ideas for his speech, and returns to the celebration. Mary watches expectantly.

... *You have full, rich lives,* he says. *The many gifts you have are multiplied through sharing them. Hold each other with open hands. Allow the water of your lives to run freely, for water gives no life until you put it to your lips. Let us drink to learn if love makes wine of water.*

Son of Timaeus

My nostrils are full of dust.
Grit is on my tongue
when he calls me.
I follow his voice.
Will I find my way back
to my belongings beside the road?

What do you want?

I barely know.
Do I want sight?
Do I want to see who I am?

I hear my unstill small voice,
I want to see,
and it is enough
to bring down the walls of Jericho,

to follow him blindly.

All

At the ever-expansive end of small existence
There is no peeping
to see what the other is doing,
no desire to be the other,
no mention of love or kindness,
no searching for identity or meaning,
no articulated purpose.

There is the opaque
differentiation of being
adult and baby
all at once,
so fully accepting,
it need not be said.
And God, if that is the word, is
the barely pink cannot-not-be,
softly pervasive
and all.

Uncomfortable love

Do you imagine 'silken tones'
when Jesus names the Brood of Vipers
or upbraids the Pharisees with *Woe to you*?
Do you imagine in the Temple, a calm

construction of the whip, a temperate
tipping of the tables upside down?
What tone of conversation freed the Gerasene?

Additional material

What volume in *Get behind me, Baal*?

What cadence in belittling words
to a woman – not a Jew –
who was prepared to be a 'bitch'
for her daughter fallen sick?

Jesus was not disturbed by anger,
by its rights or wrongs,
about discomfort in the face of it,
because what he learned from life

was that God had let him shout
when his values were in strife
and his neediness was rife
(or when he'd rather have a wife).

Contemporary culture
muffles voiced frustration.

Be spared your abyss.
Write poetry like this!

He sees and knows

In the crowded synagogue,
Jesus and his friends are slowed
by a man struggling
to free his hand from the folds of his robe.

As Jesus looks at him, the man
feels wrapped in many eyes.

A voice disarms the jostling crowd,
What law permits healing on the Sabbath?

Fear and pity seep from the silence.
Jesus replies, *Would you*
rescue from a terrible fate your only sheep
on the Sabbath day?

The protester raises his fist.
But Jesus turns towards the man

and speaks*: Stretch out your hand.*

The man stretches out his hand,
sees it as suddenly useful.

The protester gathers his clutch
to put a contract on Jesus.

I watch a once-holy Pharisee
wither into darkness.

Season Three: Compassion

Twenty-four hours

He was a fine financier
computing numbers,
record-keeping
in his head, knowing
what was owed to whom,
settling disputes between parties
socialising with monied people
born or self-made winners.

He loved the work
though he straddled the knife edge
dividing appropriate from misappropriate.

He made one risky decision,
lost everything
he thought at the time worth having.
Family went to live with relatives.

In that mad twenty-four hours,
he sacrificed a once-valued friendship.
Personal gain justified it,
called it a white lie not realising
where white lies lead.

Still wearing the robes of wealth
he slid down the bank of despondency,
wading in confusion,
no longer a bread winner

but a loser feeling loss.

He was caught
with a rope around his neck.
He could have been Judas.

Serious song

Your voice is sweet and your face, beautiful (Song of Songs 2:14).

Judas!

The memory of your death
is a tangled knot.

If only you could have
pricked your finger,
slumbered for a hundred years,
long enough to quell your greed,

and if you could have
wakened to the kiss of the Prince,
the one who had sought you all your life,
you would surely tell him of your dreams,
and he would put right the lies.

And you would believe his words; his holy song –
Your voice is sweet and your face, beautiful.

God puzzles with me

Can you imagine
leaving behind the work you love;
the work that has washed your soul
and illuminated with fire
your capacity to love and hate
and every feeling between?

Why would you do this?
Why would you take a step
from known to unknown?

How can you know the time is up
and the world as you knew it is over?
How would you know
it is time to move on, to step back,
to look from afar
at the walk or run
you have patiently done?

And when you decide to move on,
is all of you going?
Have you left a piece of yourself
to be held as precious –
the grace you have been in others' lives?

Will God heal the wounds
of the lost part
from soul, mind, and heart?
Can love be taken and left behind?

Calvary

Calvary replaces Zion.
Delight gives way to derision.
No-one wants to help.
We forget the blood
on our ancestors' doorposts.
We hunger for your blood.
Our throats grow dry.
We spit rancid words
at your face and feet
on the Via Dolorosa.
Each fall opens a wound.
You could have chosen death
right there along the way.
Your blood leaves a trail
nothing can erase.

Season Four: Joyful Passion

Love letter after Skype

I Skype you.
You answer quickly.
And there you are –
earphones and a smile.
Whatever else, I don't see.
You say – *Aren't you beautiful.*

I hear the Song of Songs –
*Your voice is sweet
and your face is beautiful.*

When I am away
I think of you, imagine
being with you.
And without a single word
I am changed.

I look into your soul
as God's own.
You are Christ to me.
Gift of more
than I would dare to ask.

Mary's grace

Generous love, risen and present,
Christ standing at the door of my tomb,
calling my name,
raising indelible memories.

You let me touch you.
It helps to feel the rough and real.

You know now I remember you.

There is no hint of regret
that you have loved me –
a woman trying to be alive.

I hold you, knowing this
last embrace before all other embraces.
It is enough to last a lifetime.

I am in you, and you in me,
Christ.

Glossary

Anthropomorphic
An anthropomorphic image of a deity is an image which attributes human characteristics to that deity.

Application of the senses
In the application of the senses [121–125], a retreatant brings the spiritual senses as well as the imaginative senses to bear on a scene from the gospels or another text, through imaginative contemplation. It is as though the retreatant is actually in the scene, and can hear, see, taste, smell and touch what is happening. The spiritual senses enable a person to savour spiritual graces such as joy, delight and compassion, as well as feelings of sorrow and love. See also ***imaginative contemplation***.

Christ
Christ is not the surname of Jesus. It is the call on every person's life. This is not to say that every person must be a Christian; rather, that the role of Christ is to be a transformative and loving presence in the world. The words 'Christic' and 'authentically loving' are synonymous. In the Christian New Testament scriptures, Jesus Christ is revealed as the person who authentically understood and lived in freedom. That freedom meant he was exposed to a plethora of experiences just like people everywhere throughout history. That freedom meant he chose to be one with God though all these things, including his crucifixion. Jesus Christ called us to be Christ in the world – *'greater things than these will you do'* (John 14:12). The Christ within empowers us to live authentic lives. It is the Christ within us that helps us to rise above deadening experiences.

Consolation
The outcome of being in relationship with God, such as joy and love. See ***spiritual consolation***.

Contemplation
The word contemplation originates from the Latin, *contemplatio*, meaning view, survey and meditation. Contemplation is composed of stillness in the presence of God. In Ignatian terms, it is profound thinking and

pondering. While it might begin in pondering something concrete, or a specific memory, thought or idea, it leads to an encounter with the divine. See **imaginative contemplation**.

Desire
In the context of *Grace upon Grace: Savouring the Spiritual Exercises through the Arts*, desire is always ultimately loving communion with God, although there are various desires which are consistent with that relationship.

Desolation
The outcome of moving consciously or unconsciously away from Love so that a person's spiritual sense becomes empty or morbid. See **spiritual desolation**.

Disabling tendencies
These tendencies are conscious and unconscious. They are thoughts and actions. Bringing unconscious psychological processes into consciousness helps a person to address them in a way that is life giving.

Disgrace
Disgrace is an attitude and action that is empty of humility. It is choosing to 'go it alone' or to be out of relationship with the Mystery of God. 'Disgrace' is the experience which calls a person towards grace.

Dreambody
In the context of *Grace upon Grace: Savouring the Spiritual Exercises through the Arts*, the term 'dreambody' is used as in the work of Arnold Mindell, founder of Process Oriented Psychology. 'Dreambody is the mirror connection between our night-time dreams and our body experiences. Every dream refers to, or 'mirrors', a particular body experience. And every body experience can be visualised and usually appears in dreams. So, to work on the body, you can work on dreams. And to work on dreams, you can follow body experiences.'[1]

Ego
This is a false construction of the self which takes account of worldly opinions and values. While ego needs to develop as we grow, it can take on unhealthy proportions when we define ourselves according to it. See **self**.

---

[1] Amy and Arnold Mindell. For further reference to the concept of 'Dreambody' see webpage: http://www.aamindell.net/dreambody/

Glossary

Entrapment
The experience (conscious or unconscious) of being caught in unhealthy thoughts and behaviour patterns.

Examen
The Examen or examination of consciousness is frequently prayed at the end of each day. The retreatant begins by noting the desire for which they have been praying. For 10–15 minutes, they contemplate their movements towards or away from that desire; the way that their daily life has been drawn to Love or away from Love. The Examen prayer helps to isolate enabling and disabling thoughts and behaviours, towards life-giving transformation.

Freedom
Freedom is a release from disabling tendencies so as to be in the flow of God's grace. This kind of freedom happens as a person becomes aware of the patterns of thinking and behaving which inhibit wholehearted living, and as a result, they choose with God's help, to address the behaviours and their causes. God is the way of interior freedom.

Grace
Grace is a difficult word to describe and define. It can be used in many contexts and the common denominator is that there is some manifestation of love in it. Grace can be used in both singular and plural forms. The singular form does not mean that there is only one grace; rather it means that it is undefined and abundant. Grace can refer to loving relationship with God. Praying for graces is praying for holy desires; those consistent with loving communion in God. Examples of graces are freedom, love, compassion, discernment.

Humility
Humility is the action of following God's call in life. Humility recognises that God knows and enables one to be the person God desires to be in them.

Ignatian meditations
Although this book contains a contemporary adaptation of the Spiritual Exercises as in [19], it is also faithful to the original intention of Ignatius. His intention to foster a person's relationship with God is continued throughout his text; that intention is seen poignantly in the Meditations which Jesuit priest, John Veltri SJ, lists as:

1. First Principle and Foundation [23]
2. First, Second, Third, Fourth and Fifth Exercises [45–72]
3. Kingdom Exercise [91–99]
4. Incarnation [101–109]
5. Nativity [110–117]
6. Two Standards Exercise [136–148]
7. Three Types of Persons (Three couples [149–157])
8. Three Moments of Loving Response ('Three kinds of humility' [165–168]).[2]

The Exercises in 2 above are the five meditations on sin in Season One. *Grace upon Grace* does not emphasise sin, but rather emphasises the love of God which transforms the world from greed and degradation to communion and abundance.

Imaginative contemplation

Imaginative contemplation is a form of prayer in which scenes and characters from texts are contemplated as if they are present; the contemplating person allows themselves to be a part of the scene. Dialogue with the characters may be part of the contemplation. The scene and events which appear in the imagination may tell the person more about themselves than about the historical reality. See also **contemplation**.

Interior movements

Generally these are affections or disaffections. They might be thoughts which evoke passionate feelings of protectiveness or fear; compassionate feelings of anger or love. Whatever they are, it is good to acknowledge them and try to distinguish their source and the direction of these movements. For example, is the movement from hate to love? Is the movement towards judgment or greed?

Journal

This is a record of the retreat. It involves writing or drawing the story of interior movements. This includes thoughts and feelings about what brings life and what seems to take life away. A film journal of dance is another possible record of interior movements. See **prayer journal**.

---

[2] Veltri SJ, Orientations Vol. 1. Available in hardcopy and online.

Kardia
Although *kardia* (καρδία – Gk. feminine noun) is literally translated from the Greek word as 'heart', in the scriptures *kardia* does not refer to the heart as the organ which animates the blood supply to the body. Rather it speaks poetically of the centre and seat of life in a person. So *kardia* finds both origin and meaning in the *kardia*-life which continually awakens desire to be who we really are in the Presence of the One who knows and loves who we really are.

Love
Love is the enactment of a decision to become unified with the Source of all things. Authentic love is more than feeling various aspects of love such as joy and compassion. It is a benevolent and self-giving action towards oneself and others. This action is always transformative; always a movement that enhances all creation.

Magis
Literally meaning 'the more', *magis* refers to listening to the deepest desires of the heart and embodying them.

Mandala
A mandala is an emergent drawing, often contained in a circle. The person drawing a mandala spontaneously chooses colours and movement to express artistically the self in relationship with the Mystery of God. Sometimes mandalas are created to express feelings and thoughts about events and experiences. There are variations to the mandala form, such as the zendala and mandorla.

Mystery
Mysteries are unimagined truths. Mystery can be used as a metaphor, just as 'God' is a metaphor. Mystery does not imply that God cannot be known. Increasingly a person can become unified with the Mystery of God through prayer.

Prayer
Prayer is primarily desire to be with God, being with God and doing with God.

Prayer journal
A prayer journal is a record of daily prayer, especially the ways in which a person has been moved interiorly during prayer. See ***journal***.

Resurrection

In this book, the term 'resurrection' is not reserved to the happenings of Christ alive on the third day following crucifixion. It includes the new life which comes when we recognise and enjoy freedom from diminishing behaviour, and are empowered by the life of Christ within. Christ within us enables us to live as abundantly and fruitfully as Jesus Christ. Resurrection is the life to which all people are called.

Savouring prayer

In the presence of God, a poignant moment from a previous prayer is contemplated again, so as to deepen awareness and insight and draw more deeply into the Mystery.

At the end of each week's prayer, a savouring prayer relishes the ways in which God has been present. Ignatius' name 'repetition' refers to this kind of prayer. The name has been changed to denote more accurately what is intended by repetition; it is to savour, to be immersed more deeply into a previous prayer.

Seasons

The four Seasons differentiate the four different dynamics and graces through which the prayer of the spiritual exercises moves. Each season is of a different length. Season Two is the longest. (Ignatius refers to these seasons as 'Weeks' which are also not traditional weeks of seven days.)

Self

Compared with the ego (sometimes called 'the false self'), the self is the realised positive potential in a human person. Self is measured only in terms of who a person can potentially be. The self is the Christ within.

Self-compassion

Compassion for oneself is love extended to the hurt and hurting dimensions of the self in much the same way as Christ reached out to the marginalised. Self-compassion reaches out to the marginalised, shamed or disordered parts of one's being.

Shame

When Ignatius suggests that we pray for 'shame and confusion'[48], shame is guilt. In the context of psychology, shame is an experience which has arisen out of being shamed by someone else for behaviours which are unacceptable to the person doing the shaming. Shame is a feeling which can inhibit the acceptance of God's unconditional love.

Sin
Traditionally sin is seen as an offence against God and neighbour. Although this word is less common now, even in contemporary Christianity, it continues to have a contemporary meaning. It is any behaviour which contributes to the diminishment of love and abundant life. Temptation towards such diminishment is not sin. When temptations are indulged, even in private, it demeans the human person and affects everyone and everything to greater and lesser degrees. Almost all of us know serious evil when we see it. Its effects are devastating. But we are not, for others, arbiters of their morality. Judgments about another person's sinfulness might be sin in itself. It is common these days to feel guilt more about failures to act and less about actions. In any case, Love takes the long view of a person's life. Errors of judgment and intentionally evil plans and actions are, in the long view, invitations to growth in personal awareness.

Soul
The animating and energising dimension of a person generally thought to have its origins in God. In Greek philosophy, *nous* was understood to be the soul and was considered the highest intelligence and intuition in union with God. Used extensively in contemporary language, 'soul' has become an attribute of persons, places and things.

Spiritual consolation
The experience of movements which energise and strengthen a person towards love, hope and desire for service. Ignatius likens the experience of consolation to water droplets sinking gently into a sponge [316, 335]. See ***consolation***.

Spiritual desolation
The experience of interior movements which deplete a person, making them morose or lacking in self-esteem, or movements which have the character of closing a person down instead of its opposite of opening up to freedom. Spiritual desolation is the experience of avoidance, resistance, or imaging God negatively. It can be the experience of wanting to turn away from God or believing that God is turning away from us. Spiritual desolation can be accompanied by depression, but it is not the same experience as depression.

Ignatius likens the experience of desolation to water droplets splashing and dispersing when hitting a stone [317, 335]. See **desolation**.

Spiritual direction

Spiritual direction is a process in which two persons, a spiritual directee and a spiritual director, discern together the way in which God is directing and inviting the directee. The content therefore of spiritual direction is the directee's experience of prayer and how prayer and life interact. Spiritual direction is a place of prayer. A person comes to spiritual direction out of desire, not necessarily out of need.

Spiritual director

A spiritual director is a person trained (formed) in the art of giving spiritual direction. Ignatian spiritual directors are educated to understand and recognise the dynamics and graces of the *Spiritual Exercises* of Saint Ignatius. These Ignatian directors 'give' the exercises and accompany a person who 'receives' the exercises. The role of the director is not to give advice or counsel, but to be the person God calls them to be; hence each director is unique in the way they listen, support, accompany and invite the directee to grow in relationship with God. Spiritual direction is a triad of God, director and directee. The Christian director makes himself or herself available to God, so that Christ in him or her is present to Christ in the directee. Spiritual directors from religious traditions other than Christian have their unique contribution to make to the growing presence of this practice in the world.

Suscipe

Suscipe is the Latin word for 'receive'. In Ignatius' *Suscipe* prayer, he asks God to receive all he is, and for God's grace in return.

Transformation

Transformation is complete or partial conversion or renewal. Look to the context in which the word 'transformation' is used. Transformation can be about appearance or substance. It can be about changed feelings, attitudes and disposition. It usually implies a permanent change but does not imply the quality of the change.

Eight-Day Retreat

I have stilled and quieted my soul;
… Like a weaned child is my soul within me.
(Psalm 131:2. ASV)[1]

---

1 *American Standard Version* of the Bible, Psalm 131:2.

Opening words for the retreatant

Welcome to your eight-day retreat in *Grace upon Grace*. You will have your own reasons for wanting to pray these exercises. Ignatius of Loyola who wrote the original *Spiritual Exercises*[1] expressed their value and purpose when he said that they were exercises to free a person (*'soul'*) from **disabling tendencies**,[2] *so that person could live fully in loving communion with God, and hence act from that abundant love* [1][3].

The word 'God' is a metaphor

The most frequently used metaphor for the **Mystery** of life or the dynamic sustainer of all things is 'God'. It is the word I use more commonly in the text of this eight-day retreat. However, I encourage you to replace the word 'God' with your preferred word. While my desire is to be fully inclusive, certain words might jar on the senses for reasons that are unique to each of us. Discuss with your **spiritual director** any word that jars, replacing it with what seems helpful to you. If you are unsure of the intended meaning of any word in bold type, consult the Glossary.

Communion

If God is the sustainer of all things, God is in communion with us and all of God's creation. Communion is the movement to which we are called, and in openness, we find ourselves drawn to God and enabled as spiritual (whole) persons. When disruption and chaos inevitably come into our lives, communion and openness invite us to listen at ever deeper levels.[4]

---

[1] Fleming's *Draw Me into your Friendship* is the version of the *Spiritual Exercises* used in this book.
[2] Words occurring for the first time in this Eight-Day Retreat and appearing in bold, italicised type are explained in the Glossary.
[3] *The Spiritual Exercises of Saint Ignatius* are divided into numerated paragraphs: Annotations [1–20], Spiritual Exercises [21] Presupposition [22] Principle and Foundation [23] and Notations [24 and following]. They denote the generally accepted paragraphs of Elder Mullan's translation of the Autograph version of the *Spiritual Exercises*. In the present text, such numbers are enclosed in square brackets.
[4] Rohr, *When Things Fall Apart*. Email linked to online page.

God in all things and God in one thing

There are two (or more) connected premises on which *Grace upon Grace*, the Eight-Day Retreat, is built; firstly, as in the sixteenth century *Spiritual Exercises of Saint Ignatius of Loyola*, God is understood as present and can be experienced in all things, and secondly, all seemingly separate things are understood to be part of a unified whole.

God's presence

We do not have to beg God to be with us. God is already participating in both the large cosmic and small particular aspects of life. God-within-us has the potential to enable the fulfilment of an intimate and infinite journey into the reality of God. Our physical senses sometimes deceive us into thinking that the world we perceive is all there is. We are easily distracted from a deeper knowing that God is the source of all we are.

Our spiritual senses help us to believe and trust that God might desire us, just as we desire God. As we lean into this hope, we share in the experience of people from various streams of spirituality who know that as we open ourselves to God, we find God waiting in love. It seems that our deeper desires are awakened and inflamed by God's desires. If we allow spaciousness for God to be who or what God wants to be in us, we find God already present. We forget our *ego*-selves and become one with God and all things.

Is God in death, destruction and distortions of Love?

While the word 'God' and the nature of 'God' might be problematic for some, the idea that God is in all things, including destructive behaviour, is likely to be problematic for many. God, whom many refer to as Love, seems to be at odds with hate and destruction. How can God be Love and yet be in all things? How can God be in destruction, death, suffering, disaster and violence? Perhaps the complexity of this question can be explored a little by the following faith statements:

> God is always present even in our power to create and destroy. But God never desires the diminution of love. It seems that God stops neither love nor hate, but is a resistant force in the hearts of those who are victims of violence. When people behave destructively, they diminish themselves; evil punishes evil. Destruction is apparently part of ongoing creation, just as we see in nature; as a star becomes depleted of nuclear fuel, it explodes. To this point in time, cosmic life has emerged as a

power beyond destruction. On earth, God's **grace** and energy continue to bring about new abundance and life-giving **transformation**. Actions such as love, compassion and benevolence contribute to this abundance that God shares with us minute by minute. God is present even in distortions of creativity, such as when humans misuse or abuse God's creative powers. Due to such misuse, the pathway to transformation becomes more circuitous and takes longer for both the perpetrator and those whom the perpetrator affects.

Distortion and destruction are not the same thing, and God is present in both. What we perceive as destruction, such as death, is part of the natural cycle of life, death and new life (**resurrection**). While destruction appears to be the breaking down of created things, it is not their obliteration. Is anything ever totally destroyed? Resurrection and transformation (of energy from one form to another) eventually emerge through the apparent chaos of creativity, destruction and the distortion of creative power.

> The conservation of energy is an absolute law, and yet it seems to fly in the face of things we observe every day. Sparks create a fire, which generates heat—manifest energy that wasn't there before. A battery produces power. A nuclear bomb creates an explosion. Each of these situations, however, is simply a case of energy changing form.[5]

Notice what brings life to you and what takes it from you – this is a key to your evolving *self* during your eight-day retreat and life beyond it.

Music

Music is selected to support you in this retreat, but as affinity with music depends on personal taste, I encourage you to choose music which will support you at the various stages of the retreat.
- Music: Ólafur Arnalds *Þú ert jörðin* (You are the earth) on the album *Living Room Songs*. 2011.

---

5 Moskowitz, 'Fact or fiction: Energy can neither be created nor destroyed', *Scientific American*, online.

Prayer

Prayer is primarily awareness of God; it is being with God and acting with God. Your whole life can be prayer. Your presence on this planet earth makes clear that God desires for you to exist. You have already been brought into being by God. God is within you. You are able to be in the 'river' of God's desire.

As you pray this retreat asking for the grace to deepen your awareness of God in your life, know that you are joining with spiritual seekers around the globe from many traditions, or from no tradition at all.

The exercises in *Grace upon Grace* contain poetry, images and music references, as well as excerpts from texts, especially the Judeo-Christian scriptures. Poetry is the language of the soul. It is open and spacious and allows a person to enter the words with their own story, drawing meaning in ways that frequently transcend rational thought.

Although the exercises are not prescriptive, they are chosen to take you through the dynamics and graces of the retreat in ways that are compatible with everyday life. In life we experience **seasons** of abundant energy, of intrigue, of grief and loss and sometimes of heartfelt celebration, so these experiences might be mirrored in your retreat. You and your spiritual director might discern together whether you should take longer over any suggested exercise.

Your desire to draw more closely to God in your life is the main element of prayer. You will need dedicated time each day for prayer. Your spiritual director guiding this retreat will listen to you, respond to your sharing and hold the process of the retreat through the eight days. The retreat is formatted for four one-hour prayer periods each day, with five being the maximum suggested. It is also anticipated that a retreatant will pray the **Examen** prayer once each day or evening.

Desire

Each day of the retreat, you will be asked to pray for what you desire. What does it mean to pray for what you desire? Desires are not superficial 'wants'; they are deeply felt aspects of love. The prayer of desire might be the prayer not to desire something, not to long for love or beauty, not to want to change or manipulate anything. Sometimes we desire God intensely but why would we long for God when we are already inextricably united with

God? Perhaps a prayer of longing is a prayer to experience feelings that we associate with God – peace, joy, love. Although our desire might be simply to have no desire, or to pray a prayer of presence, or simply to 'show up' for prayer, the prayer is nevertheless intentional.

We are body, mind and spirit people. Although we speak of these three aspects, they form one entity. An authentic desire will never be irrational to you, (although it might be non-rational or beyond rational). When we pray in accordance with our deepest desires, we are actually moving towards union with God.

Take and receive

> God, take and receive all my liberty, my memory, my understanding, and my entire will, all that I have and possess. You have given all to me. To You, I return it. All is Yours. Dispose of it wholly according to Your desires. Give me Your love and grace, for this is sufficient for me [234].[6]

In this retreat, desires are not tangible, not material. They are spiritual. Prayer for your spiritual desires is a reminder to live consciously in the flow of God's grace. It asks you to pay attention to what is happening in your life and what life is asking of you.

So it is to the ever-present God whom we turn in undertaking the following exercises.

---

6 Loyola Press. A Jesuit Ministry. Adaptation of the *Suscipe* Prayer.

Day One

Imaginative contemplation

Today you are invited to the **prayer** of **imaginative contemplation**. Imaginative contemplation is a tool of self-revelation and self-understanding. As you allow your imagination to lead, you enter the scene of the text, positioning yourself within it, and running your senses over it. What is the place and environment in your imagination? How is the weather today? Do you notice colours and sounds? What about the smells and taste in the air? What are you doing? Who is there? Are there conversations taking place? What is being said? Are you part of those conversations? Have you noticed, for example, what the characters are like, how they approach and speak to each other and to you? How are you in relation to these characters? After you have run your senses over the scene, you might find that you can run your spiritual senses over the scene as well. This is known as the **application of the senses**.

As you write your prayer reflections in your **journal**, you are developing your contemporary gospel.

Prayer for your spiritual desires

So, what is your **desire** as you begin? You could seek to be found by God. You could ask to know God's love for you. You could pray to know God more fully. You could wonder about how God sees you. You could pray to be the person God imagined and created you to be. You could pray to know your oneness with God in a deeper way.

If you dare

to put your heart in there
it will catch fire
and when hearts are aflame
there is assurance

no more daring

> just sparks of the dream
> showering stardust
> awakening

Music
- Lisa Kelly, 'May It Be' on the album *Lisa*. Celtic Woman Presents: Lisa. 2006.

Prayer journal
Your journal is a record of your prayer each day, especially the ways in which you were moved interiorly during your prayer. Some people choose to represent their experience in art or poetry. Some choose movement and dance. Researchers today have published many books which claim that writing is a transformative tool or a pathway to awakening.

Examen
For 10–15 minutes at the end of each day, notice your desire. Are you moving towards your desire or is anything moving you away?

Prayer focus for today
The bulleted points indicate a whole prayer period.
- Psalm 131. My soul is like a weaned child that is with me.
- Luke 15:1–7. Parable about God's mercy and love: the lost sheep is found.

Find me

> In the nocturnal enclosure, sparse
> shadows and child-voice rise, calling, *Dark!*
> *Find me!*

- Luke 15:1–3; 11–32. Parable about God's mercy and love: the lost son, who returns to himself and his family.
- Read the poem, 'Prodigal love', below. Choose a line or two to ponder. (You could also choose from other poems, such as 'Prodigal Sequence' which you will find in the additional material at the end of the previous, longer retreat.)

Prodigal love

The trees do not breathe
at the end of this weary August day.
Flat, leaden air surrounds me.
My temples ache
as I recuperate from yesterday
thinking

of the prodigal mystery
whose eyes lay a satin cloak
over my unwashed shame.

I am unsure of myself –

> I know what is under the cloak,
> the tainted hands
> on which the ring is placed

but I feel pain and the spill of tears,
my father's anointing.

Spiritual direction

At your meetings with your spiritual director, share your experiences of prayer and how prayer and life interact. Sometimes you will find that your prayer experiences deepen during ***spiritual direction***.

Day Two

Prayer for your spiritual desires

What do you want? What is your deepening desire as you begin this second day of prayer? You could pray as you did yesterday, to know God more fully. You could pray to experience the love God has for you. You could pray to see yourself as God sees you. You could pray to be the person God imagined and created you to be. Could you pray to be one with God?

> *Your God is the strength in your midst. [God] will save ... will rejoice over you with gladness. In love, [God] will be silent. [And God] will exalt over you with praise* (Zephaniah 3:17 CPDV[1]).
>
> *Your voice is sweet and your face is graceful* (Song of Songs 2:16 CPDV; other versions, 2:14).

Examen

Remember at the end of each day, take 10–15 minutes to recall

- the most important graced experience of the day
- the experience which brought the greatest challenges.

Can you hear God's invitation in these things? What is emerging for you?

Music

- Ray LaMontagne (singer-songwriter), 'Be Here Now' on the album *Till the Sun Turns Black*. Produced by Ethan Johns. Advance Music. 2006.

Preparation for prayer

Using the poetic image 'Prepositioning God' as your preparation for each day's prayer, gaze on the page (with your eyes only half open if it helps) initially discounting the words, until you rest on a page position which attracts you. You do not have to know why. Stay with that position on the

---

[1] CPDV is the Catholic Public Domain Version of the Bible. This is the version used in this book unless otherwise stated. Note that chapter and verse numbers in the CPDV differ slightly from those in other versions.

page. Check the word that is closest to your chosen position. Does that word speak to you about your relationship with God at present? If not, what word might better?

Prepositioning God

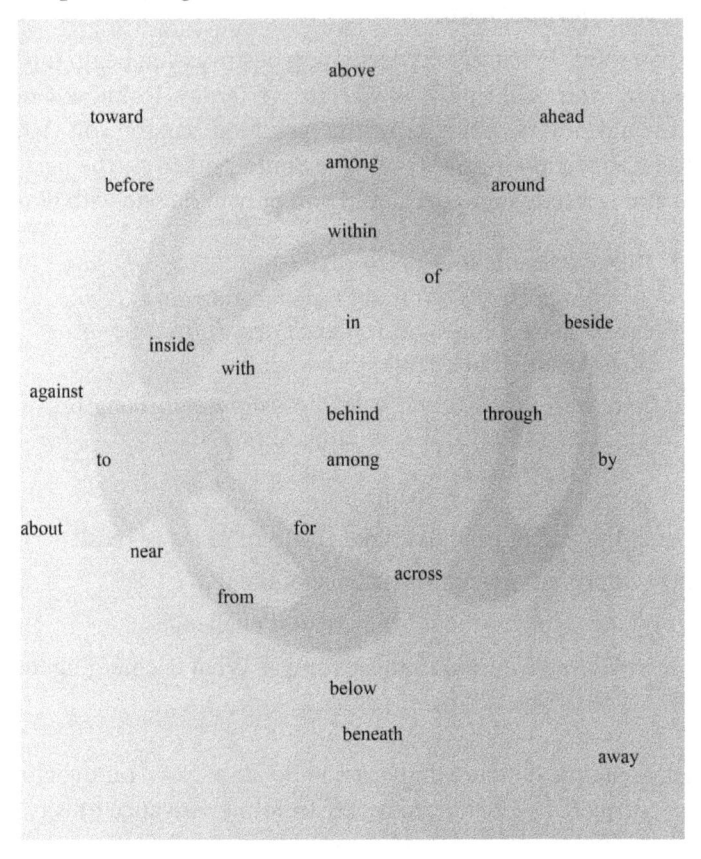

```
                          above
         toward                              ahead
                         among
           before                           around
                         within
                           of
                          in              beside
              inside
                   with
against
                         behind        through
           to           among                    by
 about                  for
            near
                              across
                   from


                         below
                       beneath
                                              away
```

Prayer focus for today
- Hosea 11:1–8. *I will draw them … with bands of love.*
- Luke 4:16–30. *The spirit of the Lord is upon me.*
- Psalm 139. *God knew you before you were born.*
- Pray over your life, beginning with the poem 'Gatherers'. Add and delete whatever 'gatherings' are relevant to you. Change the gendered, third-person language as feels relevant for you.

Gatherers

He gathered tadpoles, daisies, freckles, books, eggs,
ideas, dreams, plans, fears, hurts, shoulds, bruises,
certificates, possessions, friends, feathers, envy
joy, desires, loves.
She gathered pegs, nappies, stitches, ribbons, hair,
grapes, leaves, wood, paper, dirt,
skirts, tulle, petals, cream
worry, resentment, pounds, diets.
He gathered letters, words, calluses, burns, scratches,
courage, grief, confidence.
She gathered trust
enough to offer her gatherings
          to let go.

Contemplating your life history might clarify for you where you have come from, who you are now and who you might become. Are your earliest desires still waiting to be realised? Listen carefully to the stories emerging from your past as you ask God to help you join the dots of your life. Here are a few 'fact and feeling' questions to help:

- What were the names and ages of your parents or guardians at the time of your birth?
- Where were you born? Any medical issues? Physical characteristics?
- What is your cultural heritage? Where have you lived?
- Do you have siblings and relatives or people who have been noteworthy to you? Who is the most significant person you remember in detail?
- For what are you thankful? For what is it difficult for you to be thankful?

> Come, come, whoever you are. Wanderer, worshipper, lover of leaving. It doesn't matter. Ours is not a caravan of despair. Come, even if you have broken your vows a thousand times. Come, yet again, come, come.[2]
>
> *Jelaluddin Rumi*[3]

---

2 Rumi. Goodreads. 'Quotes: Quotable quotes'.
3 Goodreads. 'Rumi'. Rumi was a 13th century Persian poet who lived in Konya in present-day Turkey.

- List some traits or characteristics you have possibly developed as a result of your environment, your family and life circumstances. Note also the traits or characteristics which seem to have a genetic basis.
- List what you like and dislike about yourself. Concentrate on what you like, noting how well these attributes have served you.
- What role has God played in all these things? How do you feel towards God in relation to all these things?
- Note some characteristics in yourself that you don't like. Stay with this, honouring the history of your experience. Do you want a conversation with God about this? What does God say about you?
- In your journal, record your *interior movements* about these reflections on your life.

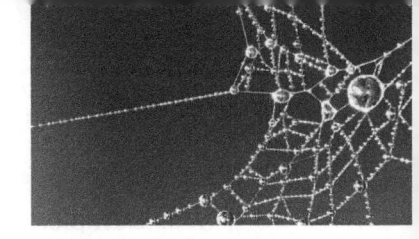

Day Three

Principle and Foundation

Would you like to pray with the Principle and Foundation of the *Spiritual Exercises* [23] instead of one of the other daily suggestions? If not, simply read them and note in your journal how you feel about these foundational statements.

Principle and Foundation. Paraphrase One

I am created to be who God wants to be in me. I am intended to bring beauty and fullness to all that God creates and empowers me to be and do. God imagined me out of love, for love. Only in love can God's full imagination be realised. Only in full communion with God can all persons and all reality know and experience wholeness.

God's world has undergone change through conscious and unconscious human action, some which seems disordered. Disorder is not flux or the polarities of everyday life but the failure to recognise and act in accordance with the love of God instilled in our hearts. This love inspires me to participate in my life-world through my personal authentic gifts. It enables me to find from the choices available to me that which will empower or disempower my life. What reason would I have to choose disempowerment? Why would I ever choose to disconnect myself from my life source?

Principle and Foundation. Paraphrase Two

God desires us and draws us closely. We experience God's desire as a heart-felt knowing and desire to be immersed in and unified with the life of God we encounter in our life-world. As we participate in God's grace, we find we are drawn by an ever-increasing desire to respond to God's personal call on our lives. To discern that call in the large and smaller choices available to us, we endeavour to stand neutrally before them committing the decisions to God. We are able to do this because many of our desires are subordinate to the deepest call and desire with which God has gifted us – to love God, learn more of the way of Christ in us and communicate the love of Christ to others.

Prayer for your spiritual desires

What is your desire as you begin this day of prayer? You could pray, as in the previous two days, to know God more fully. You could pray to know the love God has for you. You could pray to see yourself as God sees you. You could pray to be the person God imagined and created you to be; that is, the person you really are. You could pray to be open. What is your deep desire?

As you begin to pray, breathe in God's life-giving energy and love. Pay attention to how your body feels, giving special attention and care to the weaker parts. Then you might pray this promise from Ezekiel at each prayer period today:

> *I will give them an undivided heart and put a new spirit in them; I will remove from them their heart of stone and give them a heart of flesh* (Ezekiel 11:19).

Music

- Audrey Assad, 'O My Soul' on the album *Audrey Assad: Heart*, produced by Marshall Altman et al. 2012.

Prayer focus for today

1. Isaiah 45:7–13. *Creation of light and darkness.*

Vessels are hollow

> Wedged and thrown, the ball of clay
> spins, plays in liquid hands.
> Mastery of thumbs and fingers
> persuade perfect balance, symmetry,
> a rearrangement of raw earth
> rising against resistant forces
> forming a hollow the clay anticipates, desires.
> Its character awaits this test, this moment,
> every moment.

Eight-Day Retreat

The potter senses through clay-skin and
cracked and muscled hands, through
terra cotta under fingernails,
a thrilling urgent shaping,
an accelerating wheel, a dizzy race.

But she dreams:
molten clay
explosions in the kiln
sentinels on pedestals
warnings
and finally,
a settled fearless voice
heard beneath it all.

Daybreak verge,
she bypasses the wheel,
stands before studio shelves,
selects a crazed, wide-mouthed raku pot;
an ornament, hand-built, fired once.
She smiles
at each face in turn,
listens to each line and incline speak.

She prepares a generous glaze,
patient green in its hollow.

A second firing, risking, cooling.

Slowly she runs her finger-tips
over the rough and tepid surface,

raises the pot to the light,
examines its interior for cracks, flaws.

She smells the pot,
takes breath from its hollow.

She speaks into it
and from it –
an ornament no more,
a ready vessel.

2. Recall your earliest dream or memory. Recalling the earliest dream or memory, especially the energy in the characters, can be transformative. If the dream or memory is disturbing, you may share it with your spiritual director, who will help you talk about it. If the energy feels strong and fearful, consider how that energy might be transformed. If you are not ready for this prayer, put it aside for a later time. (There is no right or wrong about your decision.) Below is a process for praying about a dream:

   - Remember you are in God's presence. Recall your earliest childhood dream or your earliest memory. In your journal, write as many details as you can, noting what happened, where it happened, who the characters were, what they were doing, how they behaved, what was their appearance, how you felt towards the characters in the dream, and how they were towards you.

   This earliest childhood dream or memory is thought to have significance for your whole life journey, although once you are conscious of this dream or memory, it does not have to dictate the way your life will be. For Jung, first dreams are archetypal. They come from the wisdom of the collective unconscious. Your earliest remembered dream has energy in it, sometimes fearful and sometimes pleasant.

   - Imagine ways in which the ***dreambody*** can use energy in a positive way. Have a conversation with God about these memories, receiving God's invitation to transform the dream energy into useful energies for your life.

   You might find that the energy of the figure you fear in the dream is the energy you need to be creative. This energy is already in you. Do you believe that the future is already taking shape in you?

   - Ephesians 2:1–10. Am I living the life to which God has called me?
   - ***Savouring prayer***. Pray over anything which has emerged as dark, distasteful, bland or problematic today. On the other hand, you might ponder and savour anything which has drawn you towards light and love.

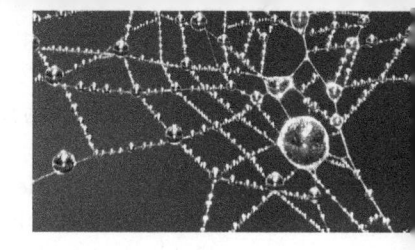

Day Four

Prayer for your spiritual desires

For what grace would you like to pray today?

What is your disposition before God; how are you with God? Has your image of God changed in any way over these days of prayer?

During each prayer period of day four, you could remember a favourite passage of scripture or a line or two of a poem or song which helps you to picture God in relationship with you. As a preparation for prayer, repeat your chosen words to savour the experience of God with you.

Examen

At the end of today, when praying the Examen, think about what might help you to flourish and experience yourself as a loving person. Are there any barriers to your freedom to give and receive love?

Music
- Audrey Assad, 'You Speak' on the album *Fortunate Fall*, Fortunate Fall Records. 2013.

Prayer focus for today
- Isaiah 54:4–10. Though the mountains fall, God's love lasts forever.
- Psalm 91. God protects and cares for you.

> **God**
>
> You speak to me,
> You are close.
> I hear as words from my deepest self.
> From here I am to be healed,
> replenished and consoled.
>
> Let me feel living waters
> splash upon my heart.

Drench me in the gift of You.
Lord teach me who I am in You.
Hold me strong
and don't let go
even when I do.

Keep my eyes open
transfixed to you and your eternal desire.
I am certain You will draw me to Yourself,
for You are Love's Self,
Who delights
in the simplest murmurings of praise
which I and he and she together
cannot help but hum.

- Jeremiah 1:1–19 Jeremiah's call. *You shall go to all whom I shall send you.*
- Exodus 3:1–10. Burning bush. *Here I am.*

Toe print

In my first step,
I put my toe-print
on God's rejoicing earth,
and all else I am
stirs in hopeful breath.

As I grow in gripping steps,
I think
my toe-print is my own.
I do not think
where it has come from
or where it is going.
I do not hear
beneath my feet, the praise
of leaves and stones
and puddles, ants and snails,
the tenor of other toe-prints
longing for our God.

Eight-Day Retreat

And as I grow in faltering steps,
I sense
within each line, each whorl,
a belonging to God's infinite labyrinth
and each step,
a trusting one of many
given just to me.

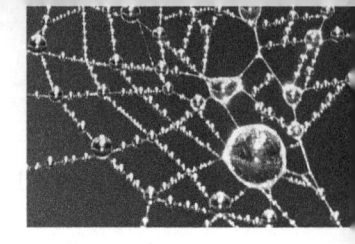

Day Five

Introduction

You are invited to ask God to enlighten you to the many ways that evil disguised as 'good' might have a hold on organisations, relationships and individuals. Ponder the ways in which human actions impact others, the earth with which we have a delicate relationship, and the whole cosmos which we are affecting even in minute ways. How might God view these events and experiences, and in turn, how do you view them?

Prayer for your spiritual desires

Today, pray for the grace to hear God's personal invitation of love to you. You might ask, as Ignatius does, for the grace of '**shame** and confusion' [48.4] at having dishonoured yourself while God continues to create and honour you. You could ask for the grace of **humility** in the face of God's unconditional, abundant love. You might ask for the grace to notice your own compassionate love or to increase your **self-compassion**.

Music

- Steffany Gretzinger, 'No Fear in Love' on the album *The Undoing*. Music and lyrics: Bethel. 2014.

Prayer focus for today

Recall a documentary film, a movie, or a newspaper item which speaks to the way in which greed or ego-driven-ness is depicted in an organisation or a person. Take some time over this. Read Luke 10:18–20. Read the scripture as poetry, and the poetry as scripture.

> **Waiting for Love**
>
> God, You are an unrequited lover,
> lovesick for me,
> waiting for the smallest hope,
> even a glance of recognition.
> You are always in love,
> waiting for me to fall in love.

- Genesis 3:1–19. The narrative of the man and the woman in the garden [51]. The man and the woman are everyman and everywoman. Focus on God as you recall your story as 'Adam' or 'Eve'. What might be a contemporary interpretation of this narrative?
- Luke 12:20. Pray for the grace to be open to notice your responses to temptations and your patterns of thought which are not life giving. Pray for the grace of self-compassion. End the day's prayer with a conversation with Jesus. Pray to be grateful.

Five wounds

Oh my God
You have arms everywhere
thrown up
in squalid air

as we violate each other.
Five bullets
nail him to ground
just to 'show the bastards'.
The fifth wound
to make sure he is dead
as dead can be.

Five bullets wound
the world,
and innocence
bleeds again.

Look at the broken body.
Feel the trembling fist on the trigger.

Each wound in him –
a wound in us.

Perpetrator and consoler,
I am powerless.

I want to live in relentless love.

Hope, forgive us.
Enable us to forgive ourselves.

- God is present to you. Remember ways in which you have loved and been loved. Visit your patterns of guilt and traps of shame. *'Nothing can separate us from the love of God which is in Christ Jesus'* (Romans 8:38–39).

Ponder the image 'Real Me' by Sieger Köder. It is a painting of a seated clown. His mask has been moved around to the back of his head, leaving his face exposed. You will find this image online.

Sin

Like water,

it seeks its own level
in cracks and fissures
and seas.
No-one knows how deep it is
until they sink to the bottom.
There

    goodness is
dragged down.

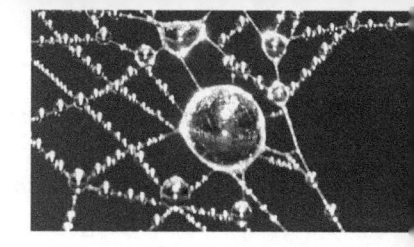

Day Six

Prayer for your spiritual desires

What do you desire? Today, you are asked to pray for the grace to hear God's personal invitation of love to you. You could ask for the grace of humility in the face of God's unconditional, abundant love. You might ask to notice your own compassionate love or to increase your self-compassion. You might ask to be united with God in God's desires for this world.

Music

- Tyler Bates, 'Santiago de Compostela' from the motion picture, *The Way*. 2011.

Prayer focus for today

- Re-read your recent journal entries. Are you beginning to notice any life-depleting patterns of thought and behaviour? However you see yourself (for example, as a struggling, flawed person on a journey, or a good person geared towards success), gauge your desire for God and pray to experience God's desire for you. Be with the present God who looks at you with generous love. Look to God as the source of all you are.

> **Becoming**
>
> The slow plough has exposed
> and plumped the soil.
> The sun gentles the surface.
> It is time to imagine
> the greening, soft hopefulness
> pushing through.
>
> I am willing to wait
> to feel the first movement of earth,
> the subtle threading of roots
> changing the deep story.

- John 21:17. *'Simon, son of John, do you love me?'* Ponder this question. You could imagine and write in your journal a conversation between you and Jesus.
- Can you imagine standing beside all that God loves, vowing your love and care? *Kanyini* (Australian aboriginal word) means connectedness. In the film 'Kanyini'[1] an aboriginal Anangu elder, Bob Randall, speaks of four types of connection which white invaders stole from the first custodians of Australia: connection to the land, connection to community and family, connection to history, and connection to 'Dreamtime' – the aboriginal worldview and spirituality which is intimately connected to place and country. The poem 'Kanyini' is a confession of guilt and shame to aboriginal Australians. You might write your own 'Kanyini' poem or story.

Kanyini

My shadow is dark across the land.
I look down,
thrust upon you
my hatred of things black,
things which obstruct
what I want.

My shadow puts me on stilettos
strutting the earth.
It makes me run,
makes me speak too fast, too much,
makes me think
I can beat its growing
presence into night.
It is never noon-day

but for 38,000 years
before Christ,
night was not night for you.
Night was as the light,

---

1 Hogan, 'Kanyini', 2006.

Eight-Day Retreat

black and blended
with the land, you belong –
keepers in the noon day
as midnight.

You are
the ochre of the land,
white witchetty grub,
honey of the ants,
emu on two feet,
hop of kangaroo.

Long the night
engulfed by my shadow, you
cannot find your way,
struggle to retrieve the ark in yourselves
when once you carried it.

It carried you.
Kanyini.
Heads held high
at one with nakedness and plenty,
drunk from the nipples of Kanyini.
Oh, mother earth.

No eyes can see.
No ears can hear Kanyini.
The heart grieves Kanyini.
The longing is Kanyini,
the spring and seasons
from which you know north and south,
west and east.

You are the land, decimated.
You are the prophet, passionate
voice in your body,
the spirit of truth
we try to discipline,
to whiten.

I listen.

The black prophet speaks
consoling words:
Lie down with your dark and flattened selves.
Be light as noon day.

- How are you, at the end of these days, contemplating Love in the face of sporadic, human love? Return to the experiential poem 'Prepositioning God' and allow yourself to enter into the place which reflects how you would like to be with God today. Then pray the gospel passage, Luke 7:36–50. The woman anoints Jesus.
- You could finish your day's prayer by choosing a few words from your journal and drawing a **mandala** which expresses those words. The mandala is a 'container' of who you are at the time you create it. Use the colours and shapes which feel free and comfortable for you.

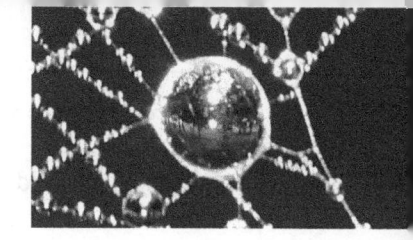

Day Seven

Discernment of your interior movements

> 'Sin is necessary, but all will be well, and all will be well, and every kind of thing will be well.'[1] *Julian of Norwich.*

Are you noticing an increasing awareness of your interior movements during your daily life? Perhaps some movements are uncomfortable and discordant, while others are light and peaceful. Note the permanence or impermanence of your interior movements; that is, which feelings are lasting and which are fleeting. Share with your spiritual director which movements lead to freedom and which movements seem to lead to **entrapment**.

Prayer for your spiritual desires

Pray for the gift of knowledge and the felt sense of being loved as you are.

Music

- Ólafur Arnalds and Alice Sara Ott, 'Letters of a Traveller' on the album *The Chopin Project*. Mercury Classics. 2015.

Prayer focus for today

- Romans 8:35–39. Read several times.

  Recall a person in your life who has loved you. Savour the experience of being loved. Imagine the capacity of God's mysterious love to look upon you with love. Stay with the experience of being loved for as long as you are able.

- The poem below might remind you of an experience of being gazed upon by love. Ask for the grace to know the gaze of Love.

  Portrait of the artist
  In gratitude to Australian artist Dudley Drew (1924–2015)

  What he sees, he sees,
  I say with the mood

---

[1] Julian of Norwich. *Revelations of Divine Love.* 'Sin is behovely, but all shall be well, and all shall be well, and all manner of thing shall be well'. Ch. 27.

of a shoeless child
naive in summer grass.

And he, poised,
like a sure-songed magpie scaling
note to note, red to violet,
touches brush on palette,
bewitched by Beethoven,
soft resonance swirling the air.
He gazes.

'What happened to you?'
pools on the canvas
in shadows not fully drenched.

His eyes dance from canvas to mirror.
Brow, like a vineyard
channeled in season,
resilient, focused,
living landscape.

He is small beside his hand
brush-stroking curves,
exploring neck to waist.
Violin passionate, tender.

And I, seen
with prodigal kindness,
am invited to be known
by the seamless heart
of Rembrandt's welcoming father.

- Ponder 'The power of nothing'.

The power of nothing

Always I would want to be mindful of you, but
it is in my soul to neglect; to forget all
but the conscious threads gathered
to serve the one present thing.

Not so with You; You do not forget
the child within You.

I think I am a poor image of You.
But I noticed this winter morning,
not one blade of grass was without
a crown of dew. You took away my breath
and kept my heart beating.

When I ache with longing
for more love than my heart can bear,
my one thought is the poetry of you

It matters only that I surrender
to the space between the words;
the nothingness defining me.

- Savouring prayer. Reread your journal, recalling the graced and disgraced patterns of your life. Bring the graces to bear on the ***disgraces***, allowing God's light to transform you. You do not have to work hard. Your desire and God's love are enough.

    Gaze

    Eyes on God.
    Two pointers to the moon.

Day Eight

Come in

I invite God inside
And find God is already there

Today, you are free to choose any material for contemplation from the offerings below or from the previous days of the retreat. This includes music or poetry or contemplation or art as a way of communing with God. Whatever you choose, you are invited to an ever-deepening consciousness of God within.

In following the pathway of your life today, notice how you feel about walking with Jesus, who knows completely what it is to be human in a troubled political and religious climate.

Prayer for your spiritual desires

The grace you have been seeking over these eight days is to know God intimately, love God more truly and intensely and follow Christ so that you live in the way God desires in you. There are several options for your focus today. Choose from the dot points below.

Music

- Audrey Assad, 'I shall not want' on the album *A Fortunate Fall*. 2013.
- Kimberly and Alberto Rivera, 'Hear the Sound' on the album *Pneuma*. RiveraSong Publishing. 2014.
- Spiritual consolation and spiritual desolation

  These interior movements have their specific character for each person. Today try to notice which patterns in your life are helpful and which are unhelpful; which patterns contribute energy and love to your world, and which patterns are obstacles to energy and love.

smog choke
fractures light
sunset

The modified haiku poem, 'smog choke ...' suggests that even our flaws in some way contribute to the beautiful persons we will become.

Just as unhelpful patterns of thinking and feeling have taken time to develop, they can sometimes take a long time to dismantle. It is helpful to take the long view and be patient with yourself in the process.

'Light dirt' is a poem about discernment. You are invited to ponder it in order to notice which principles you accept or reject.

Light dirt

You are in the right dirt if it is light dirt;
if you feel earthed, grounded, and you are steady;
if the dirt is sacred and you are thankful
that you have the privilege of being there;
walking that way, treading that path, at your pace,
using your skill, your talents;
and your life feels bigger and richer,
spacious and free. You are consoled
with God as your companion, sustainer, enabler,
and you can look in the eyes of the people you meet
to find Christ there, blessing you
with more blessing than you are giving.
You are in the right dirt if it is light dirt
and you are happy to take off your shoes,
and feel the touch of your earth-work
with nothing between you and God's desire;
finding something joyous about the mud or the sand,
something life-giving, energising.
You know you are in your right dirt when you are free
to say you are tired, that you need a break,
and that although you are skilled and good at your work,
too much of it turns you from God instead of to God;
You are in the right dirt when you discover the place within
where you are already kind, compassionate, and balanced.
You know you are in the right dirt when your heart beats
in union with God, in communion with all.

Record in your journal some important movements experienced in prayer. This is more than a record of your prayer, it is prayer itself. Through your journal, you might continue your conversation with God or gain some insight from your writing.

- Savouring prayer using a mandala.

Ignatius tells us that 'it is not in knowing much, but realising and relishing things interiorly, that contents and satisfies the soul' [2].

Drawing a mandala is useful for savouring your prayer. It is also a tool of self-expression and self-knowledge. The mandala circle is the container which holds who you are in God. The contents might appear abstract or literal. You might use a mandala as a way of deepening the graces of your prayer from any day in this retreat.

- Prayer-poem

Sustenance prayer

Reveal to me your power, God.
Inspire me by your creation
The universe, moon, planets and stars.

Reveal your presence.
Activate my memory of all that is good.
Help me to see where hope grows.
Show me seeds of kindness,
exchanges of joy,
moments of courage.

Reveal your vulnerability.
Let me see you Jesus,
Christ incarnated,
in my neighbour
in myself.
Nurture love and compassion in me.

Give me this day my daily bread
so the best of me can grow.

Amen.

- Pondering possibilities and two leadership styles.

  Consider the first scenario:

  Imagine a scenario, a place, an historic period in which a good leader is trying to exercise leadership with kindness, offering full participation to others in set goals and outcomes. The pivotal goal is dominance in a competitive environment. This leader invites you to relinquish everything for the cause. You have two choices available – you can say *yes* or *no*.

  If you say *yes*, you will share the benefits of success just as you have shared in the labour towards that success. If you say *no,* however, you will be unwelcome and ostracised. Imagine standing before this leader being offered the opportunity. Who is there as you stand before the leader seeking your response? What is the conversation like? How are you responding? Will you say *yes* or *no*?

  Consider the second scenario:

  The second scenario is similar to the first except that the leader is Christ Jesus, having gospel values and expecting holy outcomes. The goal is to work towards overcoming inequalities at every level of life. If you say *yes* to participate in his labour, love becomes the milieu in which all thoughts, words and actions occur. If you say 'no', you will walk away knowing that the invitation is always open to you.

  Imagine Jesus as a loving leader. What might love look like? Could it look like an aboriginal elder practising a spirituality in which all belong to each other, to shared history, ancestors and progeny, as well as to country which all share? This practice is in opposition to a democracy in which status, wealth and possessions are distributed and owned according to, for example, country of birth, education and influence. What else might love look like?

  Do you recognise these opposite models operating in your life or in our world? What might a world underpinned by love look like? What are your desires to contribute to a world underpinned by love? Who would be your leader? If you say *yes*, what would you offer such a leader?

  Prayer: Glory be to Creative God, to Jesus Christ, Leader and Lover, and to the Spirit of God companioning us in all of life. Amen.

- Continuing with the prayer on leadership styles, pray with the poem 'The call'.

    The call

    It is quite simple really. We are called to love –
    to compassion for the dismissed self,
    to help others to love themselves,
    to companion the unfolding of love –
    the union of self-giving and self-fulfilling love.

    How one does this, matters little
    for love is above all things, in all things.
    Love purifies and embraces all things
    until all things are indistinguishable
    from the love which permeates them.

    Is God speaking to you?

    Speak with God about what happened in your prayer.

- Luke 1:26–38. The Incarnation and the Annunciation. Imagine how God's loving presence in the cosmos impacts all things and brings about the totality of creative life that Love was intended to bring. Ponder the divine Mystery's creative imagination in Jesus Christ's entry and presence on earth in Israel.

    Read the text of 'God-with-her' twice. The first time is a simple reading for meaning, and the second time, try to become a part of the narrative. Then put your text down and let your imagination take you to the province of Galilee and the details of the place where Mary received the angelic vision. Notice the people, place and conversation.

    God-with-her

    Mary draws back when Gabriel appears.
    Confused, Mary forgets
    she longs for love, for God
    who offers more than she has ever known.

    But Mary returns to herself.
    Her heart leaps in God's embrace.

She no longer feels the boundaries of herself.
She is stilled in the eternal moment.
There are no words
to speak the way beyond
all other ways of being one.

Gabriel, blessed confidant of God's desires,
you recede as Mary says 'yes'.

Bearer of the promise,
what happens in your heart
as you witness her grappling heart?

When you are satisfied that the imaginative contemplation is complete, consider how it was for you. How did you feel towards the characters? What thoughts did you have? Was there anything new that emerged from this narrative for you? Was there any familiar pattern of response that is jarring or consoling for you? What might you want to share with God? Can you listen to what God might desire for you? Do you want to have a conversation with Mary or Gabriel? How do you want to respond?

Finish the prayer in the usual way, noting always what has disturbed you on the one hand or, on the other hand, brought life to you. Would you like to offer a prayer of gratitude?

Prayer: Glory be to Creative God, to Jesus Christ, Leader and Lover, and to the Spirit of God companioning us in all of life. Amen.

- Luke 1:39–56. The visit of Mary to Elizabeth.

    Suddenly aware

    Mary visited Elizabeth,
    and the child in her womb
    leapt for joy.

    Suddenly conscious
    of faith and heritage
    brought down through centuries.

    Discernment is an easy thing
    when love leaps.

Post Day Eight

Today is a day to re-read and savour your prayer experiences of your retreat. One way to do this is to write creatively. I am suggesting a method which helps people to write their personal poem. Many people feel intimidated by poetry and especially by the suggestion that they write their own, so I will take you step by step through the process of creating a word image of yourself. Take an A4 sheet of paper and draw an image like the one below.

- From reading your own journal, select a phrase which moves you in some way.
- Write these words in the middle of the flower.
- Ponder the words in your heart until another word or phrase comes to you.
- Write these new word(s) in one of the petals.
- Return to your initial phrase in the centre of the flower, and wait upon God again to give you another word or phrase to write in another petal.

There is no need to edit your words – leave them as raw entries, even if you do not understand them yourself. Repeat this exercise until you are satisfied with what you have written. Together, the phrases in the flower form the basis of your poem.

- Now write these phrases and words in any order, under each other as you would in writing a list.
- Add or subtract words as you please.
- Read your whole poem and give it a title.

You now have a word-image or poem about yourself at this point in time. Reflect on it. Write in your journal how you feel in relation to the poem. Allow God to speak to you through the poem. When your poem is finished, you could draw a mandala which represents your poem or the graces of the retreat.

Bibliography

Alberici, Emma. 'Whipping up fear to sway Brexit vote', *The Drum*, 21 June 2016. https://www.abc.net.au/news/2016-06-21/alberici-whipping-up-fear-to-sway-the-brexit-vote/7528104.

American Standard Version of the Bible.
> https://www.biblestudytools.com/asv/psalms/131.html.

Catholic Public Domain Version of the Sacred Bible. http://www.sacredbible.org/catholic/.

Eliot, T.S. 'Little Gidding', Section V, http://www.columbia.edu/itc/history/winter/w3206/edit/tseliotlittlegidding.html.

Fleming, David L. *Draw Me into Your Friendship: The Spiritual Exercises, a Literal Translation and a Contemporary Reading*, The Institute of Jesuit Sources, Saint Louis, Missouri, 1996.

Gallagher, Timothy M. *Discerning the Will of God: An Ignatian Guide to Christian Decision Making*, Crossroad Pub. Co., New York, 2009.

Goodreads. 'Rumi'. https://www.goodreads.com/author/show/875661.Rumi.

Hogan, Melanie. *Kanyini*. Reverb Films Pty. Ltd., Hopscotch Films, Australia, 2006.

Julian of Norwich. *Revelations of Divine Love*, Thirteenth Revelation, 27th chapter. circa 1393. https://resources.saylor.org/wwwresources/archived/site/wp-content/uploads/2012/06/Revelations-of-divine-love.pdf.

Levertov, Denise. 'Consent', in *Breathing the Water*, New Directions, New York, 1987.

Linn, D., Linn S.F. & Linn M. *Sleeping with Bread: Holding What Gives You Life*, Mahwah/New York, Paulist Press, 1995.

Loyola Press. A Jesuit Ministry, 'Suscipe. St Ignatius of Loyola', 2019. https://www.loyolapress.com/our-catholic-faith/prayer/

traditional-catholic-prayers/saints-prayers/suscipe-prayer-saint-ignatius-of-loyola.

Marburg, Marlene. *An Ordinary Woman*, 2nd ed., Windsor Scroll Publishing, Melbourne, 2017.

_____, *Grace Undone: Love,* Windsor Scroll Publishing, Melbourne, 2014.

Mindell, Amy, and Mindell, Arnold. 'Dreambody', http://www.aamindell.net/,dreambody/. No date available.

Mindell, Arnold. *Working with the Dreaming Body,* Lao Tse Press, Portland, 2014.

Moskowitz, Clara. 'Fact or Fiction: Energy can neither be created nor destroyed,' *Scientific American*, 5 August 2014, https://www.scientificamerican.com/article/energy-can-neither-be-created-nor-destroyed/.

Rohr, Richard. 'When Things Fall Apart', Meditation, no. 29, December 2017. https://cac.org/when-things-fall-apart-2017-12-29/.

Rumi, Jelaluddin. Goodreads, 'Quotes: Quotable quotes'. https://www.goodreads.com/quotes/79822-come-come-whoever-you-are-wanderer-worshiper-lover-of-leaving, 2019.

Simmonds, Gemma. *The Closeness of God: The Art and Inspiration of Sieger Köder*. Softcover ed., Pauline Books and Media, Slough, 2013, p. 54, 67.

Teilhard de Chardin, Pierre SJ., *The Spirit of the Earth*, 1931, http://teilharddechardin.org/index.php/teilhards-quotes.

Tylenda, J. N. *A Pilgrim's Journey: The Autobiography of St. Ignatius Loyola,* Ignatius Press, 2001.

Veltri, J., SJ. *Orientations Vol. 1: A Collection of Helps for Prayer,* 1993, http://orientations.jesuits.ca/bob/veltri.htm.

Acknowledgements

A number of the poems in this text have been published in earlier forms elsewhere. Thank you to the editors of journals, magazines and anthologies for including my work among them, especially Paul Grover who publishes *Studio* and the various editors of Spiritual Directors' International journal, *Presence*. Some of the poems are from my own collections – *Grace Undone. Love*; *Grace Undone. Encounter*; *Grace Undone. Passion*; *An Ordinary Woman* and an edited anthology, *Dreams and Desires*. In these books you might find poems to complement those I have included in *Grace upon Grace: Savouring the Spiritual Exercises through the Arts*.

Thank you to the spiritual directors who have used this material in its draft stages. You know who you are. I have appreciated feedback and have made changes accordingly. I am also grateful to those who have prayed these spiritual exercises. It is clear that you have found the spiritual exercises to be a supportive tool in your spiritual journeys. I am especially thankful to my colleague, Dr. Bernadette Miles, who has affirmed *Grace upon Grace* through the years it has taken to create – thank you Bernie for this gift. Julie Mitchell's photographs are masterful. Thank you, Julie. Thank you to my husband David, who is always supportive of my work, including that of spiritual direction and writing. The title and content of *Grace upon Grace* informs a one-year course offered by Kardia Formation Pty. Ltd. towards the further formation of spiritual directors who would like to help others in their spiritual growth through the spiritual exercises.

I am grateful to the editors and publishers of Morning Star Publishing. Thank you. You have made the process grace filled.

Printed in Australia
AUHW011915020919
316793AU00007B/43

9 780648 453864